Adventures of an HR Manager

2nd Edition

Jeremy Francis

DEDICATION

To my family, for the great support and feedback.

To past bosses and supervisors, for the many experiences that led to the creation of this book.

To current clients, for the opportunity to work with you in creating great organization culture.

CONTENTS

UPDATE:

The content is the same, I just added a new, follow-up section at the end, which links this story to upcoming books in a series that I hope to write.

I also included a number of related articles that I posted on LinkedIn over the past year, as well as a presentation from a conference.

I hope that you find them useful and that you will join me on future Adventures of an HR Manager.

PREFACE

I started this book during an intensely frustrating period at work. It wasn't that I didn't have meaningful work to do; I just needed something else to direct my energy into, and made time to write (well type) this.

It was the culmination of a number of things I had seen in the organizations that I had worked with at the time and from my own experiences as an employee as well. In just under a month, the first draft was completed. That was back in 2007.

Fast forward to 2014, when I finally decided that it was time to put it out there. Surprisingly, in the seven years since the first draft, not much has changed. My views on the topic are still the same, and having started my own consulting firm back in 2009, I have used and implemented a number of the ideas in this book with some of the companies I've worked with since then.

I've always felt strongly about the Human Resource function being the 'glue that holds everything together', and as an HR Consultant, I work every day to strengthen this capability with my clients. It is usually never an easy job. People issues are hard to deal with.

It is not only for HR Managers, but anyone that runs an organization.

This story is my attempt at showing a path towards getting it right. It is by no means the only way. It is just the one that I have used, and have found effective. Maybe it can help you and your organization as well.

1: The Panic Room

Roger was in a state of panic. He had to present the new HR Strategic Plan to the board in one hour, and he still wasn't finished with the presentation. He had stayed up most of last night pouring over facts and figures, making sure that the information was correct, but being the perfectionist that he was, he had to check it over again. And he did find mistakes. A lot of them. So there he was, feverishly adding and deleting slides, while his assistant Mary was running through the office, finding files for him, and putting away the ones he had used.

The thing is, Roger the HR Manager was only on the job for about six months, and had very small shoes to fill. The previous HR Manager was what he would call the 'touchy, feely type'. He had a good relationship with the employees, and was more of a counselor, helping people with their organizational and personal problems; but when it came to HR planning, there was virtually nothing done. Roger had to basically start from scratch for this presentation, as there was very little HR data and statistics for him to work with. The previous HR manager accepted all kinds of lame excuses from employees for late coming and absences, so the reports tracking these were not up to date, or correct. He also found a drawer full of sick leave slips- not filed in any particular order. But that was two months ago.

About a month ago, the General Manager, Mr. Sookoo, asked Roger to prepare a strategic HR plan for the company- a big picture for the next five years. He also told him that as part of the project, to focus on an HR operational plan for the next year. And Roger welcomed the challenge- after all; he had done one at his previous job. Roger had worked at a manufacturing company, similar to this one, as an HR Officer. The HR Manager at that company was competent, but ensured that his staff did all the work while he received all the credit. Just last year Roger had prepared a detailed operational plan for HR, and was part of the committee that developed the Strategic Plan- he had mentioned these things in his interview with Mr. Sookoo, and was sure that's why he got the job.

But now was time for action.

"Mary…where are the vacation statistics?" he asked without once looking up from the computer.

"Right here… I think," she replied, as she balanced twenty files in one hand, while opening a filing cabinet with the other. After two minutes of frantic searching through the papers that covered his desk, they found it. He frantically typed in the information.

Mary had been a God send to Roger. The former HR Manager kept little filing, but Mary had tried her best to bring some order to the office, and she had an amazing memory. One of the first things that Roger had to do when he came in was understand what was done in HR over the years, and Mary had been very helpful.

"Basically nothing," she had told him, "there was hardly any training done, and when it was done, it was arranged by the line managers, not HR."

By the end of the first day, Roger had had a massive headache, and wondered if he had made the right decision.

Apparently HR at the company was very administrative. It was limited to leave and benefits administration which Mary mostly did, while the former HR manager spent his time counseling employees and rubbing shoulders with the executives. Roger was accustomed to thinking strategically, and when he had looked through the company's Strategic Plan and saw little mention of HR, he was appalled.

"I think the old HR Manager was on vacation when they did that," Mary had told him. "He was usually out at that time of year."

Now back to Roger's dilemma. He had had a month to prepare the presentation, with little objective data for the past year. He felt like a student again, because he delved into the HR textbooks from his Masters program quite a few times. Mary wrote down from memory most of the eventful things that happened in HR, including a letter of recognition from a union that wanted to represent employees.

"The old manager just talked nicely to them, but never intended to do anything," Mary had told him.

Now the union was Roger's problem.

He had fifteen minutes before the start of the presentation, and was now reviewing the last few slides. In all, his presentation was fifty-five slides long, and the supporting documents took up half a ream of paper. It was much longer, but Mary had indicated that Mr. Sookoo didn't like to read much.

With about five minutes to spare, Roger and Mary raced over to the board room, which was on the second floor, with a laptop in one hand, and a pile of paper in the next. Mary ran behind him, in case anything fell. They got to the board room and it was still empty.

'Thank God," Roger thought.

He started to set up the projector; the room was unbearably cold, but he had no time to deal with that now.

In two minutes he was ready, and started to calm himself.

"Piece of cake Roger, you'll be okay... just stick to the facts," he murmured under his breath.

Mary was gone now, and he was alone in the board room. The pictures of the past directors hung on the wall, looking down at him with disapproval. Roger opted to look out the window. There he saw one of the cleaning personnel emptying bags of garbage into a dumpster in the car park, without any gloves, or a mask.

"I'll have to remember to do something about that", he said to himself.

Just then Mr. Sookoo and the CFO Mrs Hayden walked into the boardroom. Mr. Sookoo had a commanding presence. He was the son of the founder of the business, and had worked in the company from the ground up- over a span of thirty years. He had no business degree, but was well respected in the industry for his expertise and business savvy. Mrs. Hayden had been there for the past fifteen years, and not a loose cent got past her.

"Okay Roger, let's make this quick," Mr. Sookoo bellowed as he took his seat at the head of the table, "I have another meeting in half an hour."

Roger was not expecting this turn of events- he thought that he would at least have had an hour.

"O…okay Sir, just give me a minute to get my notes together."

He brain was racing, as he thought of ways to shorten the presentation. First he gave them both copies of the full plan, and a copy of the presentation.

"Mrs. Hayden, it looks like we'll be here all day," Mr. Sookoo joked, while Mrs Hayden looked at the binder before her with suspicion.

Roger could have sworn he heard her say something about how much paper he used, and how expensive it was.

He started his presentation with a preamble about how happy he was to be at the company, and all the opportunities he saw for improvement. When he realized that Mr. Sookoo seemed bored, he cut it short.

He started with a historical look at HR in the company, and attempted to link it with international trends and other similar companies in the industry. When he got to his tenth slide, Mr. Sookoo stopped him.

"Roger, this is not what I asked for."

W..well sir, I'm just giving a background to the presentation…" he stammered, trying hard not to show his discomfiture.

"This stuff isn't important for me to know- it important for you, that's why you were hired," Mr. Sookoo continued, while Mrs. Hayden shook her head knowingly.

Even though the room was cold, Roger started sweating.

"All I need from you are three things: What is the problem with my company, what you intend to do to fix it, and how much it will cost me. Can you tell me that in the next five minutes?"

Roger was able to stammer out a quick no.

"Well then, you have five days to get that together, and we will meet back here. I want the entire presentation done in fifteen minutes, and the written notes should be no more than five pages long."

With that, Mr. Sookoo left the room.

"And you better recycle this paper- do you know how much this paper cost?" Mrs. Hayden asked, as she left muttering something or the other about printer toner.

2: The Dilemma

Roger went to his office and put his head down on his desk for about twenty minutes. He had never been so humiliated in his life. When he came back down, Mary had purposely avoided him. The office gossip mechanism had already told her that things didn't go well- as she had expected. She was well aware of Mr. Sookoo's brevity, and had tried to warn Roger on several occasions.

"Are you sure you want to present all this?" she had asked him last week.

"Of course," Roger had said tersely, "if it's to be done right, he needs to see the research I used to back up my points."

She knew it would end like this. The old HR Manager had learned this a long time ago, and stayed out of Mr. Sookoo's way. He lasted because he let the GM do what he wanted, and when it was time to retire, there was no argument.

Now Roger was depressed. It wasn't the fact that he had spent all of last month preparing for the presentation- it was the fact that he didn't even get to finish it.

"How did he know I hadn't covered all the bases?" he complained to himself.

"At least he could have waited until I was done with the presentation."

After sufficient time of wallowing in self pity, he decided to get back to work. He would have to talk to his friend the HR Director. The HR Director worked for a large conglomerate, which was made up of many different companies all over the Caribbean. She had been in the field of HR for over thirty years, and was well respected on the island. Roger had worked with her briefly some years ago when he had just finished university. He had moved on since then, but they kept in contact, and she had become his mentor.

He had thought of asking her advice when he first got the project, but believed that he could handle it on his own. Now he wished he had spoken to her sooner.

He picked up the phone on his desk and made the call. Soon after, the HR Director was on the other end of the line.

"Hey Roger, how are things?" she asked in her usual cheery tone.

Roger related his adventures of the morning.

"Hmm…" The HR Director said knowingly.

"Seems like you overanalyzed the situation there, Roger," she opined.

He didn't necessarily agree.

"Well, I believe context is important. The lecturer in my Masters program told me…"

"Roger, I'm not usually one to knock academia," the HR Director interrupted, "but sometimes there is a difference between what's in text books and the real world."

Roger had to agree- nothing in his Masters program prepared him for the embarrassment that he endured that morning.

"Anyway, I suggest that you e-mail me the presentation, and you can come and see me in the morning. I'll go through it and give you some pointers," she suggested.

"Sure… just one problem, I think it's too big to e-mail," he realized as he checked the file size.

"Well, that's not a good sign," the HR Director commented. "Just bring me a copy tomorrow."

On their way home from work, Roger related to his wife the adventure he had in the boardroom.

"Well, at least you have an opportunity to fix it," she offered, realizing that he didn't really want advice.

"Well, it's not much time- I have to see the HR Director tomorrow, hope she can help out."

Having a new company car usually made the two-hour trek home in traffic easier, but today Roger felt he had only five days to prove that he was worth the car and the salary he was getting.

3: HR, 101

Bright and early next morning, Roger found himself at the HR Director's office. She was not there yet, so he sat in the reception area chatting with the receptionist. Soon after she came in, and after a quick greeting, she ushered him into her office.

"Come now, tell me about this presentation," she said, as they sipped cups of coffee that was brought in by the kitchen staff.

Roger gave a brief synopsis of what happened, and a printed copy of the presentation. After two minutes of looking through the document, the HR Director let out a knowing sigh.

"Roger, you missed the mark," she said abruptly.

He wasn't surprised to hear that, but it upset him none the less.

"What do you mean?" he asked, his disappointment showing on his face, and in his voice.

"I mean, if it were for a thesis, its great- but this is difficult to apply to business."

Roger had graduated at the top of his Masters class, in no small part due to his thesis, but now that didn't matter.

Seeing his confused look, the HR Director said, "Your theory is sound, and your notes are relevant, however it does not speak directly to the needs of the business."

Roger thought that she was beginning to sound like Mr. Sookoo.

"You see Roger, a for profit business entity exists for two primary reasons- to increase shareholder value, and to provide a good or service consistently- in other words, to make money, and to make a product that is always relevant to the consumer, so they always buy. Your presentation does not zero in on these concerns. It says why HR is important, but not why HR is important to the specific needs of the business that you are in."

He understood where she was coming from, but didn't fully agree.

"But I did my environmental scan, and I built metrics from company data…"

"But you didn't link it back to the needs of the business," she interrupted, "you didn't say why HR is the single most important thing to any business."

Roger was downcast. He really tried his best. He had spoken to managers and employees, looked at international trends and even compiled statistics on the company's performance over the past two years. But apparently he didn't do a good job of it.

"It's not that you didn't do a good job," the HR Director said, as if she was reading his mind, "It's just that the link to real business is lacking."

She went on to explain what she meant.

"Did you look at the company's strategic plan?"

"I did, but it wasn't very helpful," he responded.

"How do you mean?"

"It was all about facts and figures- very little to do with developing people."

"Well Roger," the HR Director, "that's why you were hired, to focus on the people. The CEO focus on the strategy, the CFO focuses on the finances and the HR Manager focuses on the people- don't forget that. If you want to be relevant, you have to show how the People can achieve the strategy, with less cost and even fewer resources- then you'll be the HR Director yourself before you can blink twice."

Roger liked the sound of that, but was clueless about how to get there.

The HR Director picked up a pad and paper, and wrote something down. She then handed it to Roger. It read:

"FOCUS ON WHAT'S IMPORTANT."

"That's the important thing Roger- keep your eyes on the basics."

She explained to him that he didn't need to do over the plan, just refine it.

"There are some people that you need to talk to going forward. There are three HR Managers within the Group of companies that you should meet. They went through something similar in the past, and I think their insight will help you. Then you can come back to see me after you speak to them if you wish."

The HR Director then made a few calls. When she was finished, she gave Roger a piece of paper with a list of three names and contact numbers.

"They have all agreed to see you, over the next couple of days- just give them a call and set it up."

With that Roger thanked the HR Director for her time, and headed for his office, feeling as though his life was about to change.

4: The First Meeting

As soon as he got back to the office, there was a note on his desk from Mr. Sookoo. The hair on the back of Roger's neck stood on end. The note said:

"Remember, What's the problem, how do we fix it and at what cost."

Roger would remember those words for a long time to come.

His first meeting was with the Technical Manager, later on that afternoon. This manager worked with an engineering company, and had been with there for about ten years. When Roger got to the office, he didn't have to wait long before he was sitting opposite him. He was still a young man- Roger gauged that they were about the same age, but he seemed to be a bit preoccupied.

"I hope this isn't a bad time," Roger offered, noticing the mounds of paper on his desk.

"I'll tell you, these days all the time is a bad time," the Technical Manager said, as he thumped away on his cell phone.

Roger was a bit taken aback by his blunt response.

"If so, I could always come back…"

"Oh, no no, don't misunderstand me, I'm glad you're here," the Technical Manager said, "The HR department is always in high demand around here, so I'm glad for the break."

With that he turned off his phone, and gave Roger his full attention.

Roger gave the Technical Manager a brief synopsis of his dilemma, and some idea of his preparations for the presentation.

"Guess your GM didn't like it huh?"

That was an understatement, Roger thought.

"Well Roger, the problem with most people in HR is that they only see things from an HR perspective, but not from a business perspective."

Roger realized that this level of bluntness would take some getting used to. He cautiously asked the Technical Manager what he meant.

"A business is a going concern, which means that if it stops growing, it will die," he explained.

"The only way HR can make itself relevant, is by thoroughly understanding the business that the company is in, and adding value as an internal consultant."

It sounded simple enough, but Roger was still unclear. The Technical Manager then told him a bit about his background.

He was actually a certified engineer, who had recently gotten his certification in HR and was appointed HR Manager. He had worked in the core of the business for about five years, and realized that the people problems were affecting output.

"We had situations where the rigging equipment was down, and because the guys didn't like the supervisor, they would only call when they really couldn't fix it and the client was complaining," he explained.

"I realized over a few years that all the brains in the world couldn't solve simple problems without simple people skills, and I got more involved in dealing with the people issues."

The Technical Manager explained that while the employees were technically competent, they lacked certain business acumen.

"And that was affecting the bottom line," he postulated.

Customers would complain to the supervisors and managers constantly, while the technicians in the field squabbled over jobs and the use of equipment.

"So I got very interested in the people aspect of the whole thing," the Technical Manager said, "and realized that:"

THERE IS A DIFFERENCE BETWEEN COMPETENCE AND ABILITY.

"It sounds simple, but the effects were very profound," he stated.

So he then took a look at the employees under his watch, and wrote out a few things:

1. How long they worked for the company

2. What skills did they have

3. What they were competent in

4. How irreplaceable they were

The Technical Manager then went on to explain that on the level of ability, which he described as the **'sense to create an output greater than the input;'** it was high among the team. Then he looked at the competence, which he described as **'the ability to add exponential value to the output through relationships with others.'** He gave an example.

"All of my engineers can calibrate specific equipment (ability), but the competent ones can make the customer feel great about the calibration, when it is done right, and in the right time- this only happens when effective feedback and teamwork occurs (competence)," he explained.

"Anyone can fix a car, but would you go back to the guy who fixed it, took your money, and walked away without saying a word and a scowl on his face? I think not."

Roger was beginning to see the point.

"You might ask- what does this have to do with your problem," he said, reading Roger's thoughts.

"Well you can add value to your enterprise by developing a plan to increase the competency of the organization."

He gave Roger a copy of a piece of paper with a diagram. It looked like this:

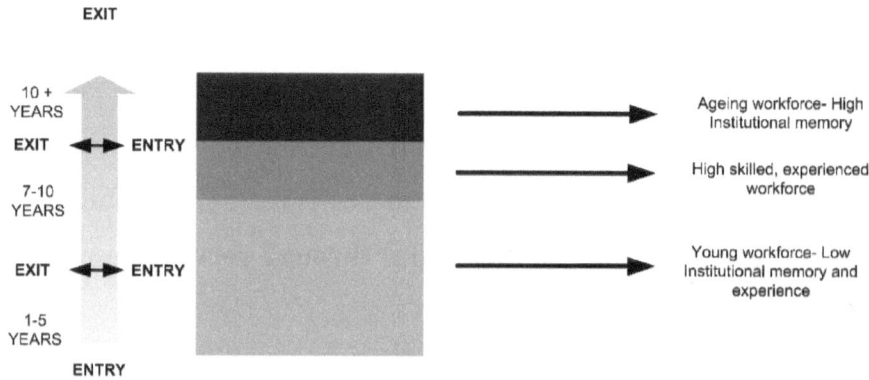

THE TALENT METER ©

The Technical Manager explained that he wrote down the names of all the employees, and using their files, identified their length of service, their qualifications and their ability.

Then he interviewed the line managers about the competencies and experience of the employees under their charge. Next, he spoke to the executive management, about the line managers, and also about some of the feedback they were getting from their main clients.

"From this, I was able to populate the Talent Meter," the Technical Manager stated, "and the output was very interesting."

In the graphical format, he was able to see three main types of employees-

1. The Head-Outs

2. The High-End

3. The Newbies

The **Head-outs** were the employees who had seen the business grow, possibly from inception, and have a huge resource of intellectual capacity on how the business runs, and an even bigger store of institutional memory, based on their years of experience.

A lot of them, while they may have professional certifications, did not have graduate degrees. This was also the group that would be retiring within the next five or so years. This group was not very energetic. They were committed for the most part; many were disgruntled because of past gripes with management and missed opportunities, and they were full of 'war stories'.

They were essentially in the departure lounge. This was especially the case in companies that have been around for some time

At the other end of the spectrum are the **Newbies**- those that have been with the company for under five years, may have the graduate degrees (or in the process of getting one), and little work experience.

This group was very energetic, made many mistakes- and spent most of their time trying to convince others why it was not their fault. They also expected to be promoted every six months, and would probably leave the company if they were not.

The **High-Ends** were in the middle. They are the small group of employees, many in management positions that have the graduate qualification, at least 7-10 years of work experience, and have enough institutional memory to make them attractive to competitors.

The committed ones were stars in their own right, whilst the disgruntled ones could be toxic.

Both had a big say in shaping the culture of the organization. In some organizations, there are only two levels- depending on the age of the company and its hiring practices.

"There are called High-End, because they are expensive to maintain, and even more expensive to lose," The Technical Manager said.

Roger hoped that he was seen in that light in his own organization.

"This group is where the greatest risk is, because they have the ability to stabilize or destabilize a company. The problem is our competitors know this as well."

So the Technical Manager used his Talent Meter to develop a program of training and mentoring, to ensure that the abilities and competencies of all groups were shared constantly.

"We teamed up Head-Outs with both High-Ends and Newbies," he espoused. "We also put together a Leadership Development Program for the High-Ends, and a Star Program for the Newbies. The Star program identified Newbies with the best work ethic, and put them through an accelerated program of training and development to get them at the High-End stage within three years.

"Since we have implemented this program, employee turnover is down, staff morale is up, and our customer ratings are through the roof," The Technical Manager explained with pride.

"Of course, other factors were responsible for this, like an efficient Performance Management System, but you will hear about that from one of the other managers you have to meet. It also did not happen overnight."

Soon after, Roger left the Technical Manager's office. His head was spinning with ideas. He was beginning to see the HR picture with a better focus.

5: Over Time.

When Roger got back to the office, Mary was as white as a sheet.

"What's the matter?" he asked, with real concern.

"Mrs. Hayden was just here, looking for you," she trembled.

"What did she want?" Roger asked warily.

"She was saying something about the overtime costs being through the roof," she trembled, "and that something drastic had to be done about it."

Roger knew that the overtime costs were a major concern- he had been reporting on the data for the last couple of months. Even Mary had worked a lot of overtime that month, helping him put together the presentation.

"Don't worry, I'll talk to her," Roger said, not looking forward to it.

He went down the corridor in the direction of Mrs. Hayden's office. He was never in the habit of going to see her. As the financial controller for the company, she had all authority with regards to the spending of company funds- as such she was very influential. She had a small office, with just the bare essentials. Her assistant waved him in without looking up from her computer. She was at her desk, poring over some financial documents.

"Roger, these overtime figures are ridiculous!" she exclaimed, even before he took his seat.

She handed him a spreadsheet, with the latest figures.

"That amount of money can pay the salary of one of the supervisors for a whole year!" she said, exasperated.

Roger had to admit that the figure was quite high.

Over the past few months the Production department had changed some equipment, and added a new process flow to making the product. Since then there has been a myriad of problems, stemming from Production, but ultimately affecting all the others, including Shipping, Purchasing, Quality Control and Accounts.

Roger was well aware of the problem, and had spoken to the Production Manager, Mr. Lewis several times about it. Mr. Lewis was sure that the problems were with the new equipment and issues with its installation, but Roger wasn't sure that the operators were properly trained.

"Roger, I know that you are working on that new HR Plan," Mrs. Hayden pointed out, "and I hope that somewhere in there is a solution to this problem, because we can't sustain this for more than three months."

He gave Mrs. Hayden a half hearted response about working on something to address the problem, but in his mind, he had no clue of what to do.

When he got back to his office, he really wondered if he was up to the task. He remembered the HR Director and the Technical Manager had said that HR has to solve real business problems, and this situation certainly qualifies as one of those.

Up to this point, he did not feel that he had a personal stake in solving this problem- as far as he was concerned, Production caused the mess, and they should be the one the fix it. But somehow that didn't seem right. If HR is to be relevant, it had to solve real business problems, he remembered.

6: The Second Meeting

Later that afternoon Roger had his second meeting, with the Assessments Manager. She worked for an IT solutions company, and had only been there for three years. Roger was impressed with the company, because they were known for their excellent customer service and product support. He was also impressed with the layout and design of the office- it felt inviting and corporate.

The Assessments Manager welcomed him into her office, and after a brief exchange of pleasantries, they began their meeting. Just like the meeting with the Technical Manager, he outlined his predicament.

When he was finished, the Assessments Manager asked,

"How do you assess your people?"

Roger wasn't sure what she meant.

"How do you assess an employee's competence in a job, and their work performance?"

Roger knew that there was no formal system at the company, but he wanted to give a better impression to this impressive manager.

"Well, the supervisors and department heads are primarily responsible for that," he explained, "they are expected to fill out evaluation forms at least twice a year..."

"I'm sure that that doesn't work out well," the Assessments Manager interrupted.

Roger had to agree. In looking at the performance files for the past few years, he found little evidence to suggest that the records were consistent, or even completed from one year to the next.

"Well Roger, that is the source of your problem," the Assessments Manager deduced, with a twirl of her pen.

"You see for HR to be effective...", she pointed to a framed card on her desk:

MEASURE THE PRESENT, TO ANTICIPATE THE FUTURE.

"You see Roger, without measures, you cannot anticipate your business," she explained, "and without anticipation there will be extinction."

The rhyme didn't escape Roger- he wasn't impressed.

"I understand where you are coming from, but how can you prove that your measurements reflect job success?" He asked.

Roger had done a course on HR Metrics, and wasn't convinced that there was a way to quantify HR.

"Well Roger, that's the difference between a good company and a great one," the Assessments Manager stated, in a matter of fact tone.

She went on to explain her role as an HR Manager.

"My job is to get the right people into the right jobs," she stated, with a smug grin.

"That's it?" Roger thought, hoping that he didn't say it out loud.

"You might be thinking that it's simple and straight-forward, but it's not."

Roger had to remember that all these people seemed to have an uncanny ability to know his thoughts.

She explained that the problems with most companies stemmed from their hiring practices, and then continued with a lack of accountability when the new hires start to work.

"We go through an extensive recruiting regime, which includes psychometric assessments, ability tests, structured interviews and reference checks," she outlined.

"It costs a lot, but our turnover rate is the lowest in the industry and our employee morale is off the charts," the Assessments Manager said with a big smile, showing Roger some graphs she had prepared.

She explained that they went through this process to ensure that there was the required job fit between the individual, the job and the organization, and only hired persons who met all the criteria. The process of outlining the job specifications and job description was very intense and structured.

"We have defined our competencies and values very clearly, based on the vision and mission of the company, and have fused these with our psychometric tests and structured interviews," she explained.

"I'd rather leave a vacancy unfilled, than put the wrong person in a job."

She explained that once the person was hired, they were introduced to an elaborate Performance Management System, which outlined clearly the tasks and targets of each employee, which was tracked by the HRIS system.

"Each employee has a dashboard, which includes weekly and monthly milestones. These targets are living targets, and are monitored constantly by the employee and their supervisor," she stated.

She went on to explain that the software was able to produce productivity reports, and armed with the psychometric tests and feedback from customers and supervisors, she is able to identify training needs and performance issues.

"We then have ongoing formal and informal training- both structured and coaching type."

The Assessments Manager told him that they were big on feedback, and the feedback was driven by metrics.

"We just don't tell someone they are not meeting targets- we show them," she grinned.

Then the Assessments Manager outlined that all this was linked to promotion and compensation.

"The metrics, plus the feedback from all the stakeholders plugs into our compensation management system, where we have various methods of rewarding the behaviors, attitudes and performance that we look for," she explained.

Roger thought that it was too perfect, and had to ask,

"Sounds great, but does it actually work?"

The skepticism was not lost in his tone.

"Well, actually yes," the Assessments Manager said, "it does because the system is fully integrated into the DNA of the company."

She explained that the process was fully supported by the entire executive, and is actually tied to their compensation. All employees use the system.

"Now mind you, it was not easy to get to this point," she hinted, "there was a lot of work, building the metrics, testing them and implementing the software, but after about two years of constant work, the system effectively manages itself, and gives us pertinent reports that help us manage our most valuable resource.

She gave him a copy of a diagram that outlined the methodology:

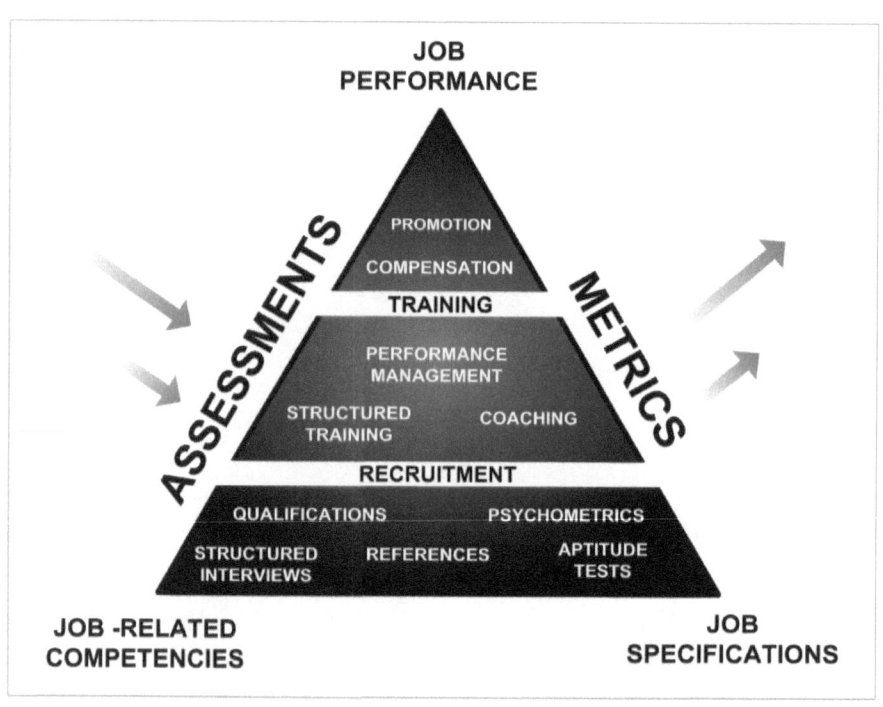

THE ASSESSMENT/METRIC TRIANGLE ©

"At its most basic level, assessments are the input, and metrics are the output for all layers," she explained.

"Not all companies can afford an HRIS, but since we sell it, it makes sense to use it."

She told him that effective HR management must be built on performance indicators, in the same way other departments are judged.

"Production, Marketing and Finance all have performance indicators- why not HR?" she asked.

Roger could not argue with that.

He went home that afternoon with a headache. He was getting a lot of information, but fitting into his present circumstance was becoming a problem. He had three more days to put together the presentation, and was no closer to answering Mr. Sookoo's questions.

7: The Restart

Later that night, Roger started putting his thoughts together. He needed to put a business case for his existence to the General Manager- at least that was how he saw the presentation. He had little relevant data to work with, the company had no formal recruiting or training policy in place, and the Performance Management System needed an overhaul.

On the business side, the company was profitable, had two major competitors locally and was dealing with the challenges of the new processes and equipment in the Production department. From what he could tell, morale was usually low- employees liked the company, but there was a stiff quality to communication and interaction.

The Management team worked relatively well together, and was made up of senior technical persons in their field. With regards to HR, it was mainly administrative and not strategic, but Roger realized that he had to change that.

He pulled out the organization chart and had a look. It had the typical hierarchical structure of older companies. He didn't think that anything was necessarily wrong with the structure, other than the fact that the organization's culture had created individual fiefdoms, called departments.

Each income generating department competed for resources and buy-in from the General Manager, so a suspicious and tense relationship developed between them. This was reflected in the behavior of the rest of the organization, as the employees took on the characteristics of their managers.

He had to note that the company worked well, but if they lost a major customer, or if key individuals left the organization, they would be in some trouble.

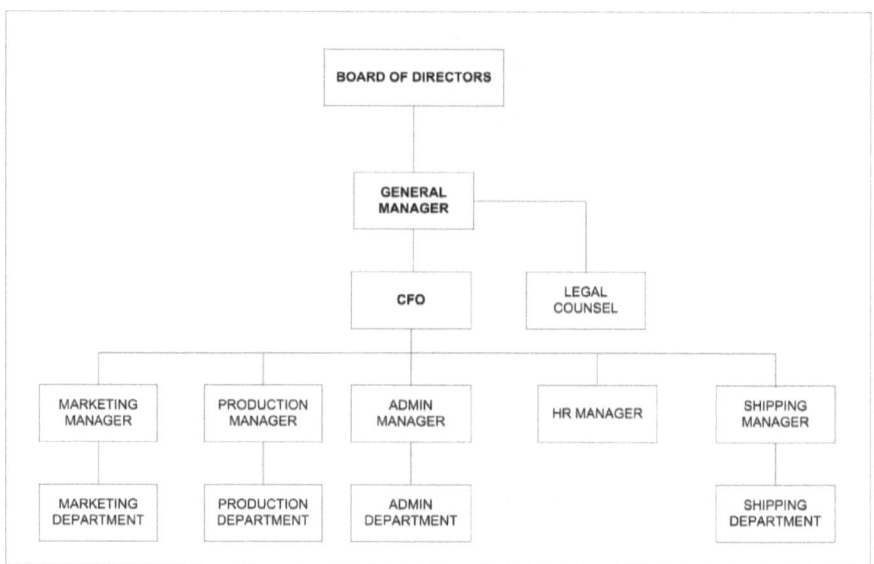

ORGANIZATION CHART

Roger assessed what the Technical Manager and Assessments Manager had told him. As he flipped through his notes some things started becoming clear. He picked up three main points:

1. Quantify the talent in the organization

2. Measure it

3. Share it

Quantify It.

He was basically unaware of where the talent and institutional memory of the company resided. As far as he could guess, it lay in the mind of Mr. Sookoo, a few of the other managers and some other employees who had been there a long time. This made them basically indispensible. Measuring it was a problem, because at present, the only way to gauge the importance of this information was by imagining what would happen if the key people were not around. Then how do you share something that was never quantified?

He remembered the Technical Manager's Talent Meter. Based on the length of service of employees, he did his own meter. Even though there was no science to the process, it had a very interesting result.

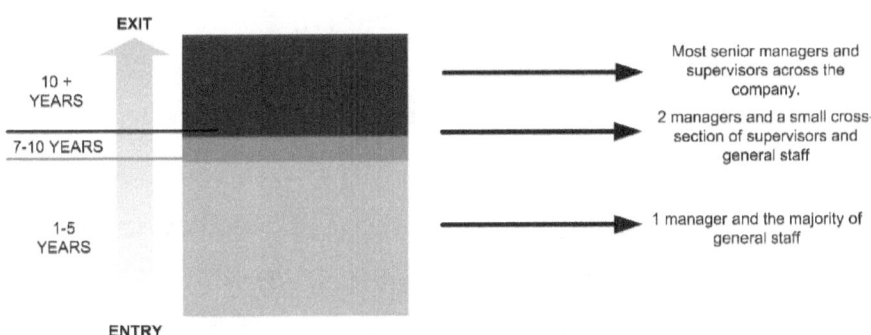

The Company's TALENT METER ©

For one thing, the middle layers were very small. Looking back, it would seem that many of the 'High Ends' had moved on- either to competitors, or out of the industry altogether. Even more worrying was the amount of 'Head Outs' who would soon be leaving due to retirement. Roger was now confronted with a serious succession planning issue.

The next problem was the large number of employees who were with the company for less than five years- including him. He also realized that many of the conflicts within departments were between 'Head Outs', and 'Newbies'. The old and the new.

There was a culture gap between those who worked their way up in the company, and those who expected that their academic expertise meant that they should be in the senior positions already. This brought up the issue of coaching and mentoring.

He then did another diagram with the years of experience that the employees had, regardless of where they worked. For instance, he was new to the company, but he worked in HR and administration for about seven years prior to joining the company.

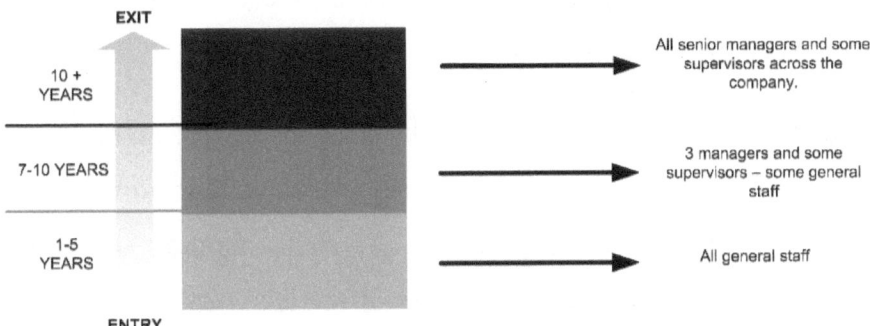

The Company's Experience Meter

He felt a little better about this one. Even though most of the employees had been with the company for less than five years, the distribution of working experience was more evenly distributed. This could mean that less technical training may be required- which could also mean that soft skill training and coaching may be more relevant.

Measure It.

Then tying this all in to what the Assessments Manager had told him, he thought of performance measures and metrics. Such a system was largely non-existent at the company, and each manager basically managed their people's performance in their own way.

One manager literally sat over his employee's shoulder, ensuring that things were done his way, while another left his charges up to their own devices, and only intervened in a crisis.

When it came to Performance Management and Appraisal, this was usually a frustrating experience, because most of the managers were very subjective and tardy with their responses.

Roger believed that this happened because there were no objective measurements, and that the appraisal was a generic form which didn't measure anything precisely. As such, bonuses and profit sharing was not an objective process. Roger had met the system as it was, and was unsure of how to address it at the time. After seeing the Assessments Manager's system, his mind was overflowing with ideas.

He flipped through the notes of one of his Masters program courses and found a diagram that outlined the components of a Performance Management System. It looked like this:

PERFORMANCE MANAGEMENT

Naturally, there had to be a link between individual and department goals and that of the overall aims and objectives of the organization. Roger agreed that it was necessary and looked lovely on paper, but he also knew how difficult it was to get such a system implemented, and working.

It also meant that a significant shift in the way managers and supervisors interact with their employees would have to occur.

Share It.

The other challenge was the return on investment on coaching and training. Apart from the fact that he would have to develop a training plan and methodology, he would have to get it past Mrs. Hayden.

Most finance officers dislike spending large sums of money on training, as the direct organizational benefit is difficult to track.

It is easier to do a cost-benefit analysis on a new photocopying machine, than a management development program. But it was very important that if the business is to thrive, that the institutional memory be shared throughout the organization, and for certain skills that are in short supply to be added. He would have to find a way for Mrs. Hayden to buy-in to the concept.

Then he thought about the problem in the Production department. Even though it affected the entire company, Roger realized that because the departments operated as silos, it was seen as only a Production department problem. Whenever it was discussed in Manager's meeting, the other managers took the opportunity to highlight the problems in Production, and how it was adversely affecting their area. None of them, and Roger had to include himself- saw it as an organizational problem that they all had a part in fixing.

He knew intuitively that because of the competitive nature of the managers, they would take any opportunity to showcase their area at the expense of the others. The effects of a silo structure, he realized.

Roger believed that a team approach was necessary to solve the problem, but was clueless about how to effect the change. He was sure that if he could come up with a workable solution, he would get the overtime figures down; then getting buy-in for training and development programs would be simple. He made a note is his diary to contact an HR consultant he knew quite well to get some guidance.

8: The Third Meeting

The very next morning, Roger had the third meeting, with the last manager on the list- the Process Manager. He had just about two and a half days to re-present to Mr. Sookoo and Mrs. Hayden, but in his mind, things were coming together. His problem now was to find a way to effect organizational change from silos to a team based environment. He was hoping that the Process Manager could help him.

"So, what can I do for you?" the Process Manager asked, as they sat at his desk.

Roger again outlined his problem, and also mentioned his concerns about the current structure of the organization. He enquired if the Process Manager experienced the same problems, and what could be done to fix it.

"Well Roger, first off we don't have that kind of problem here," the Process Manager said, "in fact we do not have a hierarchical structure at all."

Confused, Roger asked him to explain.

"Some time ago, we had reached the maximum capability of the company- we were fully mature, and innovation was at an all time low," he explained.

"Mind you, the company was doing well financially, but over time we were losing market share to our competitors- slowly, but surely."

The Process Manager explained that the CEO decided that something needed to be done, and had said something that has remained with him since:

IN A GOOD COMPANY, $1 + 1 = 2$

IN A GREAT COMPANY $1 + 1 = \infty$

"At first we were all skeptical- we were somewhat familiar with continuous improvement, but over the next few weeks, we began to understand where he was coming from."

The CEO brought in a consultant, who over the course of a few weeks showed them how synergy and innovation can be used to create exceptional results.

"We did have a silo structure, where each department had a mind of its own," the Process Manager explained, "but we have since moved to a process environment, where cross-functional teams work as units to achieve incredible results."

Roger had recently read in the local newspaper a few weeks ago about the company and an award it had received for innovation and entrepreneurship. He had actually cut out the article, because he found it remarkable that such a company existed in his environment.

"For about six months, we set up a series of cross-functional teams across the organization- made up of people with different skill sets and areas of expertise," the Process Manager outlined.

"Since I was responsible for HR, I had a great deal of involvement in the set-up of the teams. Each team was given a series problem statements, based on complaints we had gotten from customers, and also a copy of the company's mission and vision. Each team was given a mandate-

SOLVE THE PROBLEM, AND THEN RELATE THE SOLUTION TO OUR MISSION AND VISION."

The Process Manager went on to explain that at first, it was a rough experience. People were largely unclear of what they had to do, and quarreled over the minor details. After about four weeks of this, the consultant came in and gave them some direction.

She outlined a five step approach:

1. Problem identification

2. Problem solving process

3. Educate and communicate

4. Plan for implementation

5. Implement and follow-up

He then gave Roger a breakdown of the process they initiated.

The Process Manager stated that firstly, they defined the problem, using a specific framework of how the issue affected the customer.

Then the desired outcome was identified- which would usually mean a satisfied customer.

Objective measurements were identified, which were used to prove that the change worked.

Implementation steps and the resources required were stated clearly.

After that, a team was selected to implement the solution. This diagram outlines the process:

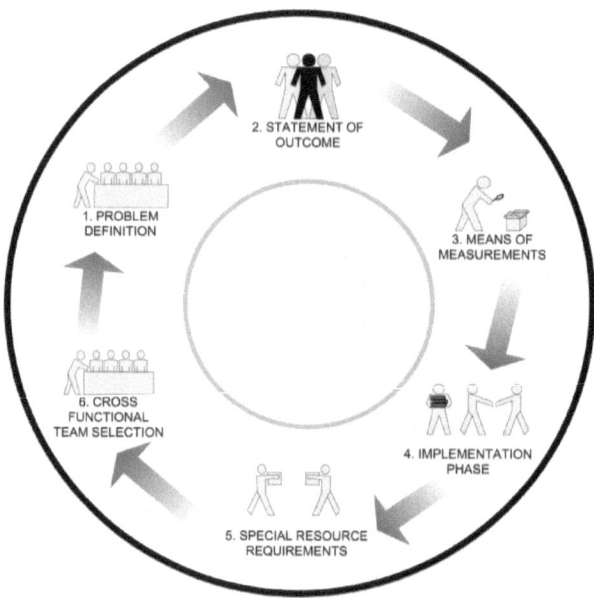

PROJECT PROCESS

"Over the period of a few months, we realized that the 80/20 rule applied," the Process Manager stated.

"80% of our problems were caused by 20% of our key processes."

He went on to explain that, as a company, and led by the CEO, they tackled these processes- but then a new problem emerged.

"We realized that our hierarchical structure was preventing us from achieving a firm resolution… we were being more effective, but efficiency was being affected."

As a result, a decision was taken to reform the organizational structure, and formalize the cross functional teams.

"We formed permanent cross functional teams, with rotated membership and leadership.

These teams met at regularly defined periods to tackle customer and other service problems. Not only were problems identified, but the possible solutions were also presented to the management team. The management team then analyzed the most cost-effective and efficient solution, which was then implemented. An incentive and reward structure was put place to encourage team development and problem resolution, and members of the teams included all employees- from managers to the shipping clerk."

The Process Manager explained that HR was responsible for coordinating the work of the teams, and implementing the reward structure. And wherever training and ability gaps were identified as barriers to solutions, recommendations were put in place to mitigate these issues.

"I know it sounds great, but this took more than a year to set up-there were many setbacks, and involved a lot of extra hours. It led to a change in organizational culture, and the usual reporting structure within the company had to be changed. Employees were now empowered to make certain changes independently, and managers had to spend more time managing the performance of their people. It was a large re-engineering effort that is still underway, but our metrics show that it is working," the Process Manager said proudly.

And indeed it was, because the performance of the company has steadily improved since the process begun.

By the time Roger left the Process Manager's office, his head was swimming with a mix of problems and solutions. He needed to find a quiet place to organize his thoughts and structure them properly-he had the answer, but the path to get there was still a bit unclear.

9: Eureka

The morning of Roger's presentation had arrived. He had spent the remainder of his time, after meeting with the Process Manager in relative seclusion. His only contact had been with the HR Director, who helped him work out the finer points of the plan. Unlike the last time, Roger was very calm and confident. He was armed with a great plan and execution strategy, and was thrilled with the possibility of having the opportunity to roll it out to the rest of the organization.

Mary was very curious of this new plan, but he did not let her have a look at it, nor asked for her assistance. She seemed hurt, but he knew that she would have a big role to play in its implementation. He would show her after.

He got to the boardroom early, and set up the presentation. He had done only ten slides, and the handout comprised only four pages. He knew that would make Mrs. Hayden very happy. He thought of the old presentation, and realized just how far off the mark he had really been.

Soon Mr. Sookoo and Mrs. Hayden entered the room, and with them was the Corporate Secretary.

Mrs. Hayden picked up the handout, and was visibly impressed with its size and the fact that he used recycled paper to print it on.

"Okay Roger, the floor is yours," Mr. Sookoo said, as they all took their seats.

Roger began his presentation by paying tribute to the legacy of the company, and its role in the development of the economy and its employee's lives. He stated that it was important for the company to survive, and in order to do that, its orientation had to shift.

He outlined some of the threats that faced the company, such as:

1. Local and international competition

2. Cost of raw materials

3. Loss of key employees

4. Capital expenditure on new equipment

He painted a picture that highlighted the fact that the company had to evolve, to keep pace with the environment, and his presentation would outline how:

PHASE 1- STRATEGIC VISIONING

Roger planned to start with a weekend manager's retreat, where the management team would focus on the following:

PART 1: Translating the company's Vision/Mission and operational plans into specific performance objectives for each department.

Although this was already done to some measure, Roger wanted it to be drilled down further, with a focus on the customer. For this he would prepare a number of scenarios, based on actual customer issues, and it would be the task of the team to analyze them through the lens of the company's vision.

He would even invite a key customer to deliver a presentation at the retreat, to highlight issues related to service.

For the last part of the retreat, Roger would outline the HR Plan for the organization. This plan had three main components:

1. Talent Management/Training and Development

2. Performance Management System

3. Institution of a Cross-functional Team environment

PART 2: Cross Functional Team Assignment.

Roger would then form two ad hoc teams to deal specifically with the problems now facing the Production Department. With the help of a consultant, both teams will develop solutions for the problem plaguing that department.

The aim of this was to introduce the concept of process teams, but also to show the managers what could be achieved when they worked together.

PHASE 2: THE HR PLAN

Part 1: Talent Management

Roger outlined a project to do a skills inventory of all the employees in the organization. This would involve a survey to obtain up-to-date records of academic and professional certifications, and would include an analysis of current job functions and the specific competences required for these jobs.

Additionally, Roger pulled out a series of competencies and values from the Mission and Vision of the organization- words that outlined the type of individual that the company needed in order to succeed. Here are some of the competencies he listed:

1. Ethics/Integrity
2. Team Orientation
3. Leadership
4. Innovation/Entrepreneurship

With the help of the management team at the retreat, these terms would be further defined, to state what they meant for the company. They would then be circulated to the rest of the organization.

Through the talent management exercise, a technical skills and competency framework will be identified for each level within the organization. To do this, psychometric assessments, surveys and interviews will be used, but not at all levels. Once the skill identification process was complete, training programs would be designed to tackle both the hard and soft core areas. Additionally, employees with proven competence and experience in technical areas would be assigned to a small group of trainees as part of a formal mentorship/coaching program.

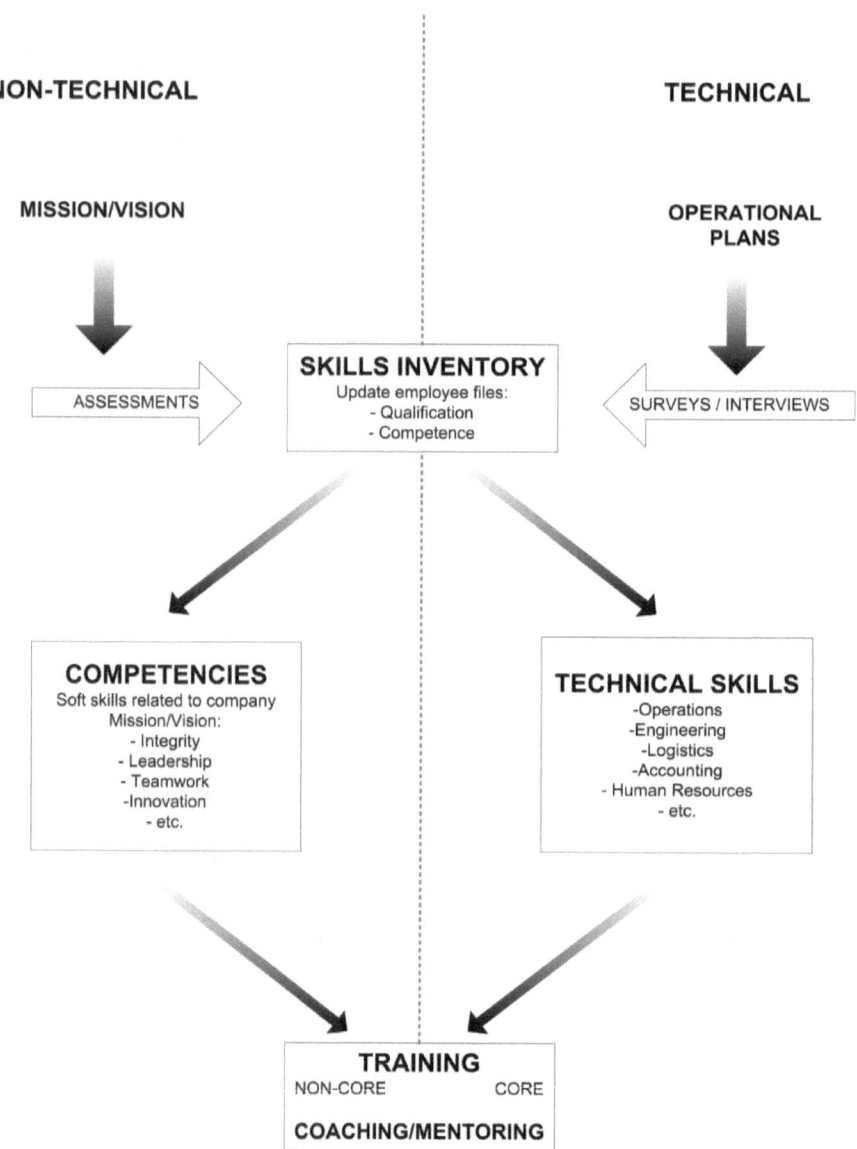

Part 2: Performance Management

Using the talent management framework, Roger would then revamp the Performance Management System. He showed them the diagram from his textbook, but added company specific information to show his point.

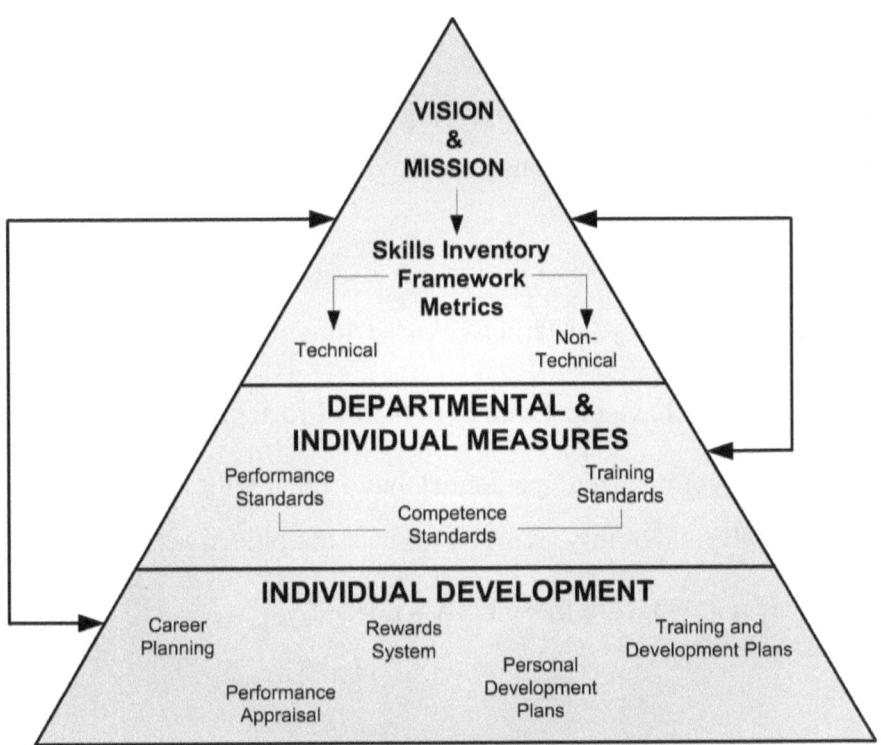

PERFORMANCE MANAGEMENT FRAMEWORK

His idea was to use the skills inventory framework as the basis for the Performance Management System.

That coupled with the competencies identified by the Management team and the Operational plan objectives would be used to develop the following:

1. Performance Standards

2. Competence Standards

3. Training Standards

Based on the yearly objectives Roger would ask the management team the following questions:

In order to achieve your targets-

1. Do you have the required personnel to achieve them?

2. Do your current personnel have the required knowledge, skills and ability (KSA's) to meet the objectives?

3. If not, what are those KSA's needed?

Based on this information, a survey and psychometric assessments of persons in key positions will be developed. And of course, these will be done in consultation with all key stakeholders.

Once this is completed, a number of procedures will be put in place, based on the metrics outlined:

1. **Performance Appraisal:** The forms are to be re-done to capture the Skills Inventory. Also the scheduling will be standardized.

2. **Career Planning:** Now that appraisals are standardized, the data collected will be used to do formal career planning for employees, and will assist in succession planning.

3. **Reward System:** With a formal system, rewards and compensation policies can be more objective. They can also be directly linked to performance objectives.

4. **Personal Development Plans:** Linked to career planning, employees will have the opportunity to identify development areas based on their appraisal and assessments. Plans can be both job related and based on personal goals.

5. **Training and Development Plans:** A formal training program will be set up for the company, and will be informed by the Performance Management System. This will include shorter technical based courses, and longer, competency based programs.

In order for the Performance Management System to be successful, its implementation was to be tied to a new incentive program. Along with their financial targets, managers would be expected to use and maintain the system- this would be tied to their bonus packages.

Part 3: Process Improvement

The third aspect of the plan includes the breakdown of organizational silos, and the introduction Process Improvement Teams. Coming out of the strategic retreat, and the team that will be formed to brainstorm a solution to the Production department's problems, Roger also proposed to set up a series of cross functional teams to tackle customer and organizational issues.

It would start with a customer feedback survey, which will give an idea of the issues that the teams should tackle. The teams would be made up of employees from across the organization that will meet on a scheduled basis to discuss and brainstorm solutions to problems identified by customers and other stakeholders. The teams would receive training in process improvement, and will have a reward structure to support their problem-solving work. As the teams develop, they will be formalized, and the aim will be to have process teams replace the hierarchical departmental structure in time.

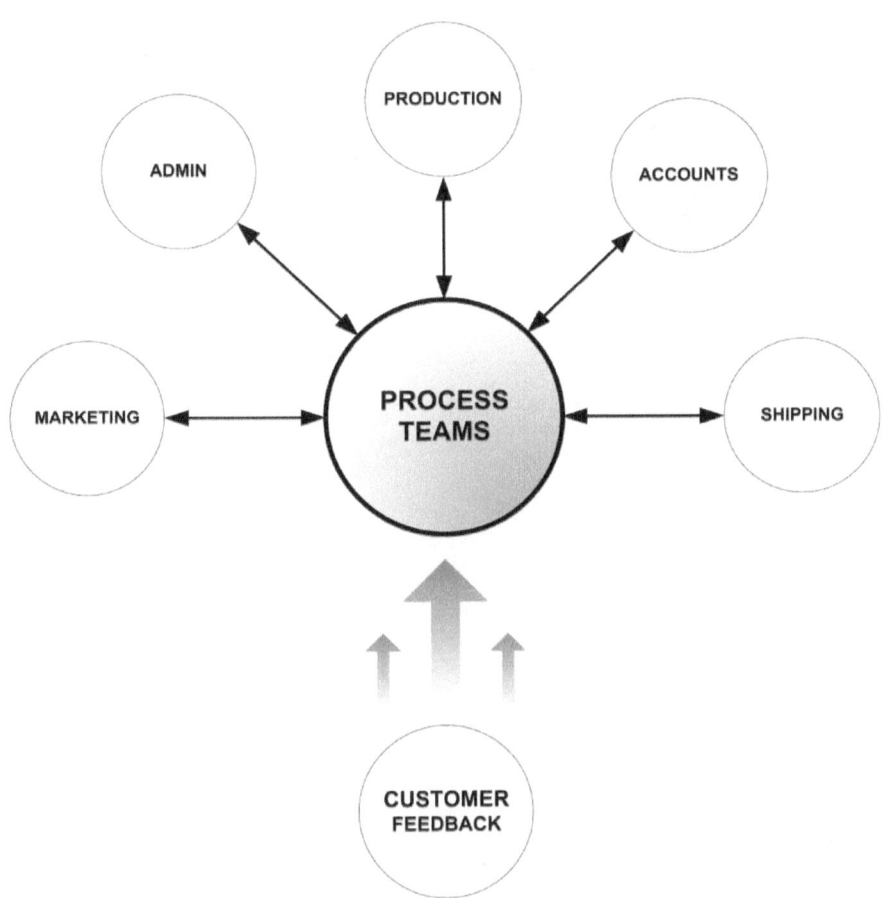

PROCESS TEAM COMPOSITION

Roger believed that this process is essential to increasing innovation and teamwork within the company, and the work of the teams should not be limited to solving customer issues.

As part of the process, the teams can look inward- at ways of making the company a great place to work. Projects such as a daycare for employees, health and wellness programs and car pooling were some of the ideas that he put forward.

The Overall Strategy

Roger's last slide was a summary of all that went before:

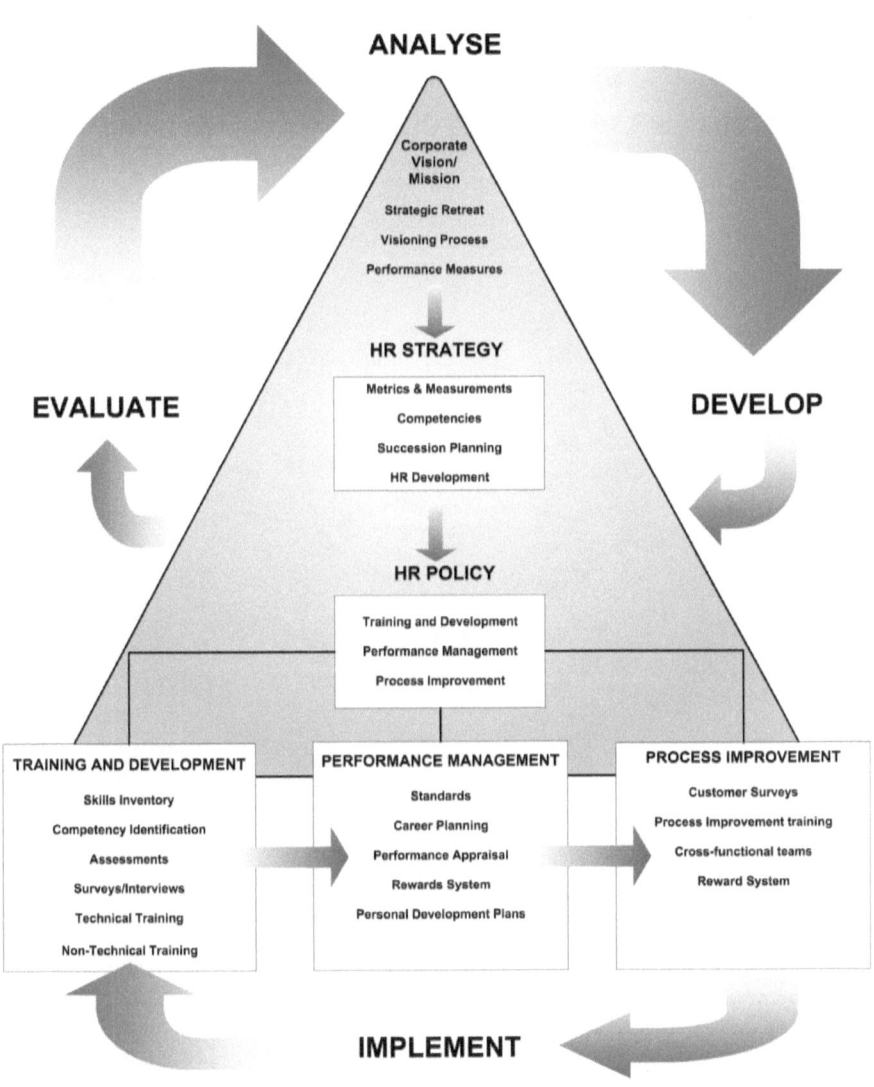

He spoke about the cascading effect- from Vision to Implementation. He directed their attention to how special the workforce was, and how important it was to value them as human beings. In forty five minutes he was finished. Then the questions.

Mr. Sookoo didn't seem to mind that he went over the time limit he had set.

10: The Aftermath

Mr. Sookoo thanked Roger for his work, and the wonderful presentation. He said it was exactly what he was envisioning. He believed strongly in the people in the organization, and thought that the plan outlined clearly how they were to be treated. In principle, he had no problem with the plan, and was sure that the board would endorse it.

However, he needed to impress on Roger that at the end of the day, he had a company to run, and shareholders to please.

He needed to know:

1. How much such a plan would cost?

2. How long it would take to implement?

3. Did he have the resources to get it done?

Roger was ready for this. He felt that most of the preparatory work could be done from within- with the current staff. He estimated that he would eventually need to hire an additional HR Officer, and that Mary should be promoted to that position as well.

He intimated that he would oversee the implementation of the plan- in particular the Performance Management System. The HR Officers could oversee the Training and Development plan and the Process Improvement teams.

In terms of cost, he stated that apart from the new hire, it would be difficult to determine at this point; however he introduced a metric to guide the process.

He stated that in relation to training, the cost per employees should be no less than 10% of their annual salary. For instance, if Employee A made $50,000.00 a year, he or she will be eligible for at minimum $5,000.00 in relation to training.

Other costs related to the use of consultants will have to be factored in. He also noted that his salary, as well as that of the two officers should be added as well.

He noted that the plan would be expensive to set in motion; however he was certain that the benefits had the potential to be phenomenal.

He made reference to the companies whose HR managers he met with over the past few days. All three companies were leaders in their industry, with sound financials. Roger believed that this was in no small part due to the emphasis they have placed on their people.

In terms of implementation, he put forward the following timelines:

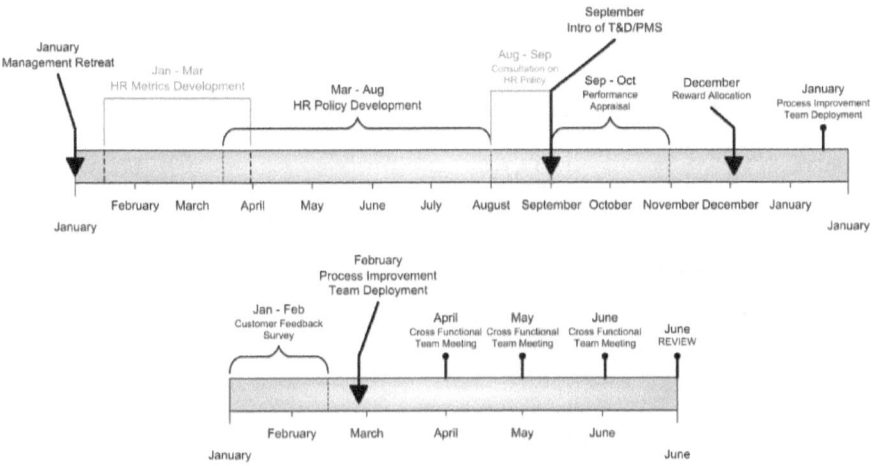

IMPLEMENTATION SCHEDULE

Roger believed that a year and a half of focused work could lead to the implementation of the HR Strategy, and that within three years, the company would see the tangible bottom line results based on the HR interventions. At the end of it all, even Mrs. Hayden seemed impressed; a bit skeptical, but impressed. The overall feeling of the meeting was that the plan was necessary, but the concern was Roger's ability to get it done.

He assured them that over the last few days, he lived nothing else but this plan, and was fully committed to seeing it through.

A couple of weeks later, Roger had to do the presentation to the board. He was in a better position with a figure on the implementation costs, and tied himself to performance metrics to ensure accountability remained with him.

Within a few days Roger received the go ahead for his plan. He was elated, but knew that the next few months would prove his worth as a **Strategic HR Manager**.

Epilogue: How Did it Go?

Two years had now elapsed since Roger made his presentation. He sat in his office, looking over the performance figures for the last year. There had been a marked improvement in several key areas, and he was proud of the fact that the Process Improvement Teams had really picked up. Over the past year, they were able to tackle real customer and organizational problems, and it had the added benefit of making the participants cross-functional, as they interacted closely with their colleagues in other departments. In fact, some people were even transferred to other departments, and were adding significant value.

The introduction of the Performance Management System was actually very troublesome at the start. As a result of the high level if mistrust among managers and staff, and the subjectivity of the previous reward system, it was a difficult sell. The managers as well had a lot more to do, in terms of spending time doing performance appraisals and developing career plans for their departments.

In fact, a few employees and one manager left the company, because they were not willing to work in the new environment. But the majority of staff was hopeful, and was willing to give the system a try.

The managers were the first to admit that with the introduction of the system, communication within their departments improved, and it was easier to manage the performance of the department with the new metrics that were introduced.

The coaching and mentorship program also assisted in making communication more widespread throughout the organization, and employees now worked together to solve difficult problems.

He remembered the problems in the production department. Coming out of the management retreat, they had all agreed that it was everyone's problem, and for the next few weeks, all the managers put their heads together to ensure that production and delivery schedules to customers were achieved.

Within five weeks, the situation had been rectified, and it was clear that teamwork solved the problem.

Mary was now the assistant HR Manager, and they had hired an HR Officer, who spearheaded the development and management of the Performance Management System.

Roger himself managed it all, but he was directly involved in the Training plan, and the Process Improvement teams. He had found it necessary to vary some aspects of the original plan as he went along. Flexibility was important. They had a long way to go still, but things were falling into place, and the financial figures showed that it was working.

He was now often called in by Mr. Sookoo and the other board members to give advice on various business decisions, and soon it was only natural for him to take a seat in Executive Management.

Roger made it a point over the last two years to understand the industry in which he worked, and was able to put all the HR practices within the right context of the business. He was not only seen as an HR expert, but as a business expert.

As he was about to head into a meeting with Mr. Sookoo his phone rang. On the other end was his friend, the HR Director.

"Hi, how are things?" Roger said, as they exchanged pleasantries.

"Great, need your help," she began.

"I just hired a new HR manager for one of our subsidiaries, and would like him to speak with you."

Roger agreed without hesitation, as he had once been in that position not too long ago. The HR Director had sent a few people to him over the past few months, so he could share the story with them. He had learned a lot from the people around him, and had no problem sharing his knowledge. It was a story where HR turned around the fortunes of a company- it was the story of a Strategic HR Manager.

THE FOLLOW UP

It has been five years since Roger implemented the system at the company. He was no longer an HR Manager. In fact he was no longer with the company. Four years ago, Mr. Sookhoo had asked Roger to take the helm of a newly acquired subsidiary. His job was to get the company aligned with the rest of the group, and implement the same system there.

It had taken two years of very intense and hard work, but the team rose to the occasion and the project was delivered on time and on budget. Roger was on course to have a great career with the Group. But something was missing. Even though he thoroughly enjoyed the experience of building HR systems, and ensuring that quality standards were met, it became increasingly difficult for him to motivate himself.

After taking a bit of a break from work at the end of the second project, he decided to make a change. So after many talks with his friend the HR Director, and with Mr. Sookhoo, Roger decided to leave the company and set up his own HR consulting business. It was always something he wanted to do, but other things always got in the way. Like fear. As much as he knew he was capable of it, the fear of going out on his own was overwhelming for a long, long time. But the things that he was able to achieve over the past few years showed him that it was possible. And after much planning- and agreement with the wife, he resigned and set up his own HR consulting company.

His first client was the group of companies that he had just left. His former employer was now his client. And whist his familiarity and knowledge of the company was an asset, Roger did not expect the difficulties of now being classed as an 'outsider'. He no longer had ready access to all the necessary information- even getting paid was a problem at times. He soon found that he needed to find business elsewhere.

He also realized that as much as he loved the HR field, there were aspects of it that he did not enjoy. So he decided to focus on the areas that peaked his interest- namely Performance Management and Management Development. Slowly but surely, he built up his client base and reputation in this area- and a few years in, it was beginning to pay off.

Running your own business requires an entirely different mindset from being an employee, Roger realized, and he struggled a bit with motivation issues in the first year or so. When you worked for a company, there were so many things that were done for you. Things like getting paid on time, services such as health care and even car maintenance. Now he had to manage all of those things on his own. The company was still too small to hire an assistant, so he battled with the paperwork as best he could.

But that was a few years ago. He was now in a better place, and there was a greater sense of continuity with his projects and clients. He was even able to increase his skills in key areas, by travelling abroad and doing specialist courses- something he never had the time- or the inclination, to do before. All in all, it was a positive and eye-opening experience.

Soon, he got a lead that Capital Investments were looking for a performance management specialist to help them revamp their performance system. Some time ago, he had met their HR Director, Tracy at a conference, and they struck up an immediate friendship. He was hoping that his proposal submission would be favorable, because he had heard good things about the company; and from what Tracy had told him, it was similar in many ways to the experience he had with Mr. Sookhoo and his companies.

How did it turn out? Well you are going to have to stay tuned for future instalments in this series- the Adventures of an HR Manager.

The company has a lot of Policies? It's because you Lack This.

April 2, 2015.

The one reason why companies get employee engagement wrong is that the leadership lacks one thing- empathy. Trusty Wikipedia defines empathy as: '*the capacity to understand what another person is experiencing from within the other person's frame of reference, i.e., the capacity to place oneself in another's shoes.*'

This my friends does not come naturally, or easily. In fact, the arrogance- and even hubris that comes along with being promoted to executive management positions tend to kill whatever traces of empathy some people may have.

80

Here are a few things that a lack of empathy leads to in organisations:

1. Stringent policies and procedures that penalise employees for minor infractions (like late-coming).

2. Punitive performance management systems that are big on the stick, and light on the carrot.

3. High-stress work environments that are deadline driven

4. Poor customer service- the focus is on getting it done, not necessarily on getting in done in a way that pleases the customer.

When executives are unable to empathise with workers- that is, see them each as unique individuals, and not as a homogeneous, lazy group- they can develop the ability to make decisions that don't punish Peter and Paul- when John was the real culprit.

As an example- John often comes to work late. So instead of addressing the issue with John, the department head sends out a blanket memo to all staff, stating that late-coming will not be tolerated. John assumes that the manager is talking about Jane, because last week, she came in after him twice. Jane gets upset because in the last six months, she came to work late twice (last week) because her son was ill. The manager feels justified that she 'dealt' with the situation- John is unaffected because he assumes that he was not the target, and Jane gets demoralised because she thinks the memo is unfairly targeting her.

Empathy would have solved this problem because, and the empathetic manager would have known that Jane was late because of her son. She would have known this because Jane would have been comfortable coming to her with the problem because she is a good listener (as all who possess this skill are). John, on the other hand, would have addressed his late-coming, because this manager would have spoken to him directly, on more than one occasion about his late-coming, with the aim of finding a solution. And where none was forthcoming, the necessary corrective action would have been addressed to him directly.

I have worked in organisations, both as an employee and as a consultant where the management believes that staff are lazy and give only half the effort. Employees, on the other hand, believe that management is stingy and demanding. As a result, the battle lines are drawn, and no one trusts anyone.

Management responds by instituting draconian policies (like warning letters after coming to work late more than three times). Employees respond by withdrawing their enthusiasm from work (by doing exactly what is asked, and no more). Nobody wins. Least of all, the customer.

And while both sides are guilty of a lack of empathy, but it is management that must take the lead on this. A lack of empathy leads to an environment where trust is absent. All decisions- even those that are beneficial to employees are viewed with suspicion. Every act by an employee that is not in line with 'regulations' is seen as a breach of the established order. And it goes downhill from there.

The solution?

Listen to your employees. And not only to what they say but listen to what they do. For this to happen, you have to turn your focus away from the bottom line (sometimes) and focus it on THEM. This takes a lot of effort if you are not accustomed to it.

Give them the benefit of the doubt. Do not assume the worst. Have regular meetings to deal with issues within the department. Stick to your word. In other words, *lead the company, stop managing it.*
As easy as this sounds, so many companies get this wrong. And will continue to do so. On the other hand, the company that gets it right will not only have happy employees but a healthy bottom line. Who wants to be first?

HR Department, You're Fired.

February 23, 2015.

As management consultants, we do get a lot of criticism for being expensive and not adding a lot of value. This may be true for some. Before I became one, I had my own bad experiences with consultants, to the extent that when I started my practice, I didn't like to refer to myself by that title. The fact that the name of my company is Beyond Consulting speaks to that because I always felt that there was more to it.

But I have to tell you, now that the shoe is on the other foot, our usual employers the HR department, sometimes make me want to give them the boot as well. But that would be frowned upon when you consider that the customer is supposed to be always right.

But it is OK to fire a customer, and it happens quite a bit. Here though, I am going to deal with some of the things that HR departments do that eventually lead to project failure and the mandatory blaming of the consultant.

The 'I Need Advice' trick.

So you have this work project and are not quite sure how to execute. So you call a consultant that you know has been trying to get work from your company. In a very friendly tone, you ask for advice, and they give it freely, hoping to build rapport, and eventually get a foot in the door for a job. You take that advice, craft a scope of works and put it out to tender with your preferred list of service providers... and do not include the one that advised you in the first place. You eventually give the job to his competitor. Not cool HR.

Just pay someone for their expertise in developing and writing projects, or develop the skill yourself. Leading someone in and then dumping them is a bad romance.

The 'I don't know what I want' ruse.

Well, this one isn't always a trick. Sometimes HR does not know what they want. They think they do, but in some instances, they don't. So they tell the consultant what they think they want. The consultant listens, hears what they want, and tries to advise the client. The client thinks the consultant is just trying to make more money. They say no. The consultant, not wanting to turn down a payday, delivers what the client said they wanted. It does not go well. The consultant is blamed and does not get paid. Truth be told, the consultant in this instance has to share the blame- sometimes you have to know when to walk away from a job.

'Rolling in the Creep'.

Though my pun on Adele's hit song is really bad, the effects of scope creep are worse. I start the project with one mandate. Six months later, the mandate has changed three times, and the project is off schedule. And the only part of the contract that the client is not willing to let 'creep' is the cost. So twice the work for the same pay. This is related to point 2 above. It is times like these that you wish time machines were invented.

'That wasn't in the Scope' cop-out.

So the project is almost at an end. But to get it done, a previously unforeseen issue has to be addressed. You discuss it with the client and agree. When the time comes for the project closeout and payment, the client 'forgets' this aspect of the project, and refers you to the original scope and contract you have signed. The additional work is not covered. Their problem is solved, but yours is only now beginning.

Project Schedule Russian Roulette.

You agree on the start date and duration of the project. The week before you are due to start, the client keeps calling to change the dates. The first two times were cute. By the tenth time, you are pulling your hair out because the client fails to understand that you do have other clients, and you can't amend your schedule at the drop of a hat. It pisses off other clients when you end up changing agreed upon dates with them.

So you try to work in a clause where the client has to pay for your time when changes and cancellations are made at short notice. They get mad. You get cussed out from other clients when last minute changes are made to their timelines. The one shot in the gun has the consultant's name on it.

The fact is, a lot of these problems could be avoided if HR was clearer on what they want to have done, and consultants were less eager to please.

I've also found that while many people in HR are well qualified, they lack experience in project planning and execution. And they also lack the political clout to challenge decisions made by the higher-ups that can jeopardise a project.

Quite frankly, I always try to deal with the head of the organisation first, and work with HR as part of the implementation team, though this isn't always possible.

I'll work on the professional standards of consultants HR if you work on the issues raised above.

Psychology vs HR in the Workplace.

June 30, 2015

This realisation came to me very strongly today, as I deal with an issue with a client. I have opined in the past that although I am an HR consultant, I'm not crazy about the field of HR. In fact, my first degree is in Psychology. And although I've done post-graduate studies in HR, most of my qualifications are still on the side of Psychology, rather than HR. Why?

I've noticed that in the workplace, the understanding human behaviour is way more important than regulating it.

May sound like heresy to some. But my experience of HR over the years have led me to believe that as a business practice, it concerns itself more with the process and structure of human relationships in business, rather than the People aspect of the business. And that's OK. Which is why I think that a lot of the criticisms of HR is unfair. HR is there to (only), provide a safe and functional working relationship between employees and the organisation. But employees expect more. They expect HR to defend them against bad bosses. Unfair business practices. Be a shoulder to cry on. But technically, human resource is a function geared towards bringing order and stability to the resource that is human. And that is not always in favour of the human. End of story.

And the image of psychology as couch-bound therapy, and Freudian discussions about Oedipus (though sometimes relevant), are not part of the discussion.

Issues such as recruitment, retention, employee engagement and training and development are very important processes that have to be managed effectively- to ensure fairness and so that the organisation maximises its investment in its people. And these issues are very much psychological in nature and require that lens as well.

And this is why I have a love/hate relationship with it.

The understanding of WHY people do things, the motivation and the desires of individuals and groups is usually lacking- and is where having HR persons with a background and appreciation for Psychology can help. By its very nature Psychology is the study of human behaviour- and Occupational/Industrial Psychology is the study of Human Behaviour in the Workplace. And that gives it the advantage.

Policies, procedures and structure is great. If we were solely dealing with machines and inanimate objects. I've often seen decisions being made- even by HR departments, that have not taken into consideration the human impact of those decisions. And it makes me sad. Because a lot of great potential is lost, and some intelligent and driven people become de-motivated and lose their spark in a myriad of forms and procedure.

If your HR department is made up only of HR specialists, consider adding someone with a background in psychology, or better yet, occupational psychology. This will be of particular positive impact in your hiring and talent management practices- especially if your company uses psychometrics, assessment centres and competency-based interviewing practices.

Most management degrees gloss over these topics, but they are integral to many HR processes. As such, I do see a few companies missing out on the full potential of these tools because their staff lack a full understanding of them. My psychology background allows me to add that value to client engagements- all the better when I meet someone in the HR department that speaks my language.

The Future Office (and it doesn't have an HR department).

January 19, 2015

I may or may not have written a post about my lack of love for the field of Human Resources. But the problem I have with HR has little to do with the field itself, and more to do with how it is practised in many companies.

I firmly believe that many aspects of the HR function can and should reside within each department, with the HR resource acting as a consultant, to give guidance, set policy and do trend analysis.

Because of the highly specialised nature of the modern economy, we have pigeon-holed so many aspects of our world, when a more team-based and collaborative culture would be more effective. This trend is catching on though.

And what would an HR-less company look like? Let's look into my crystal ball and see...

In the not so near future, I get to work and swipe my pass to gain access to the office. The panel on the door gives me a greeting, asks after the welfare of my family, and tells me what is on the menu at all the restaurants in the vicinity of the office. It also tracks the time I get to work- not to see if I came in late, but as an input to my efficiency report.

What is that you may ask? It is a program that matches my work time to the achievement of my monthly goals. If I achieve these goals in less than the projected time, I get that time back- or I can credit them towards my vacation.

The time could also be used in other ways, for instance, I can come in an hour later, and get that run in before I get to work. If for any reason I don't complete my tasks within the suggested time (which is an amalgamation of people doing similar tasks), then a notification goes to me and my team leader, for us to meet to discuss how I can be supported to complete it. Other team members can assign some of their 'free' hours to me, in exchange for credits that could be used for a grocery list of items.

As I get to my desk, my intranet page pops up. It gives me a graphical report that shows how I am progressing on my objectives. I no longer have to be subjected to performance appraisals, as my team leader can see how I'm doing on his dashboard in real time and we meet weekly to assess goals.

My dashboard also shows how many days vacation I have left, who else has vacation, birthdays and the like. It also has aa activity counter to show how many steps I make in the office each day. At the end of the month, the most active person gets a prize. The sensor in my pass measures my movement within the building. As part of the Wellness initiative, the company promotes us being active during and outside of working hours. More active employees gain credits for activities such as running, swimming and cycling, and the company pays the race registration fees for up to five events per year, for those who want to race. The company also has a fully sponsored team that participates in events.

I click on the training tab on my dashboard. I have a session carded for next week. A couple of days after that, I have a review session, where I have to do an hour-long presentation on what I learned and how I'm going to implement it with my team. **It will be over lunch. That I have to buy.** Those are the rules. Training is based on the allocation of a quarterly budget, that is managed by each team leader. He or she is responsible for allocating the necessary training to all team members. On his dashboard is an ROI indicator for said training, that they are responsible for, to the next line on management.

A couple of weeks ago John was fired. He had some DUI's (Disciplinary Unit Indicators) and had been missing his targets for several months. His objectives were allocated to the rest of the team, but our collective efficiency reports showed that we would miss our quarterly targets if he were not replaced. As a result, a request to find a suitable replacement was sent to the external recruitment firm, with details of the job scope and responsibilities for the position. A detailed psychometric profile was also sent, outlining the personality types that would most fit within our team. Which reminds me, I have to find time to complete my online assessment before the end of the week.

At the end of the work day, I log out of my workstation. It stays in the office. We are not allowed to take work home. All client calls are forwarded to a help desk, who in turn notifies a manager if action is to be taken before the next workday. All calls to our work cell phones are routed to the help desk after hours. We also can't access work emails after hours. That is family time, the CEO said. Work time is to get work done.

Now back to reality. I've covered some or most of the major tasks undertaken by HR. Here, it is done within the department, or through the use on technology. Do you think it is possible? And is it already becoming a reality in some companies?

HR vs HR... Internal, or Outsource?

February 3, 2015

The HR Consultant vs the HR Manager. It is the quintessential battle between Batman and Superman: without the capes, gadgets and admission fee. Can a company exist without an internal HR department? Can HR be outsourced? Let's start the discussion.

I just wanted to give a practical example of how HR can operate as an internal consultant and the fact that that person does not have to be an employee of the company.

As a consultant, I provide HRM services for a few of my clients. In reality, I act as the HR Manager, giving guidance on a range of matters. I have been involved in recruitment, promotions, disciplinary matters and firings, as well as performance management and training. I visit these clients for a few hours per week, on a retainer basis.

This gives me the flexibility to work with other clients in a similar capacity. Additionally, the fact that I can work for several clients simultaneously means that I can leverage the experience of one for another while maintaining confidentiality. In several cases, I have arranged meetings between my clients who were facing similar issues.

The most important aspect of my job is that I spend 90% of my time with the respective CEO's, discussing business matters. HR matters do come up from time to time, but the core of the discussion is about the business. And to me, this is the most important function of a consultant or an executive, to give advice, and share expertise to keep the business moving forward.

Naturally, my focus in these discussions focuses on the people, and in effect, all discussions are painted with an HR brush. But we hardly ever discuss HR issues on their own- only about how they can assist in solving a business problem.

One of the obvious advantages of this kind of arrangement is the fact that I don't get cabin fever. What is that you ask? I do not become part of the company culture that tries to explain away issues and problems with comments like, 'that's how it's always been done.' In other words, I'm not an employee, so I don't lose my objectivity. It also allows me to ask questions that employees may be afraid to ask, or who assume they already know the answer.

When HR is also an employee, it sometimes becomes difficult to maintain a 'safe distance' from issues when you become a part of the culture. It is also difficult to raise objections with the person who signs your cheque. It is the same person who signs my cheque, but it is easier for me to walk away. Plus, the CEO's I work with like the fact that I don't always agree with their point of view and challenge them often.

I do this primarily for companies that are too small to have a dedicated HR Manager, but too big not to have someone focusing on HR issues. You may think that this system cannot work in a large company with far-flung employees. But it can if HR is decentralised and each working group or team has an HR resource attached that reports to a central authority- the internal HR consultant/executive.

Even in the companies, I work in, I insist that an administrator is hired to coordinate some of the days to day HR activities that are necessary. There are tasks I will not do, and someone needs to tie it all together. And as the company grows, they will have someone who can easily transition into a full-time HR role.

I have seen large companies with sizable HR departments still get certain things wrong. If communication is a problem, no doubt the HR team would also be a victim of it. There are so many aspects of the HR function that can be outsourced, making the delivery of such services more efficient and cost-effective.

And no, this is not a plug for independent consultants and consulting firms. If there weren't a market for our services, we wouldn't be here. If it weren't an option for some, then so many current HR professionals would not be leaving the relative security of full-time work to establish a private practice.

In many companies, HR has long lost its role as an employee advocate. In many companies, HR has become the sword of management. It's natural when HR is considered as a cost Centre, striving for limited resources. Freeing the HR department from the shackles of the organisation may be the thing that makes it relevant for many again.

The Rubber Stamp Effect: and how HR can get out of it.

January 16, 2015

I have a confession to make: I'm not a big fan of the field of HR. Normally this wouldn't be a big deal, but I happen to be an HR Consultant. Yes, I know. But in my defence, I find it a lot easier consulting to the heads of organisations about HR issues, than to be running an HR department myself. Hats off to all of you out there that do it- that takes a lot of effort. That being said, there are a few reasons why I do have an issue with some HR departments- be it a company that just has the one HR Officer or the firm with a 10+ sized department. It is a similar problem that some executives have as well, though they may not be able to articulate it properly. Usually, they just keep HR out of major business decisions. Then yell at HR to fix it when it goes badly.

Employees too have a like/hate relationship with HR. I didn't use the word 'love' because let's face it, who loves HR? You know, those guys and gals that monitor how many times you are late, are always pestering you to fill out weird forms, and don't enter your vacation request on time. *Those guys.* But in the main, the role of HR is mainly misunderstood, and surprise, surprise- mostly by people in HR.

Here are some of the reasons why HR ends up being just a rubber stamp, and things you should do to change that.

They don't know the Business.

I have worked with a few different industries, and rarely have I met an HR professional with practical experience in the said industry.

Yes, the majority of HR professionals is well schooled in the academics of HR and may have loads of practical HR experience, but I have found that some of the most effective persons in HR have more than just a passing knowledge of the work that the company they work for does. In a few rare cases, these people worked in other departments at the core of the business before transitioning into HR.

The benefit? They have a real sense of the business issues- and people issues within the company, because they would have experienced it themselves.

It is unreasonable to expect that HR professionals will become experts in the work that the company does. But what I would expect is that some effort should be taken to get as deep an understanding of that work as possible, so that they can provide better insight as to how HR policies and procedures can support the growth of the business. It will take time- and real interest. And if all else fails, you could always ask someone from the Operations department to join the HR team.

Too Non-technical

Yes, I know that it takes a lot of training to become an HR professional. Because there are so many facets to the field, it is important to get some specific training in some areas, especially if you are a generalist.

For those who work with psychometric assessments, you should become certified. If you do coaching from time to time, there are a lot of courses and certifications that you should look into. And if a request comes in for something that you are not familiar with, don't be a hero and 'try to help out.'

You may make a bigger mess of things, and further reduce the credibility of HR. Consultants are around for a reason. And no, not just to take your money in exchange for obscure advice. They can add technical expertise where it may be lacking. But it is even more helpful that if I, as a consultant, is talking to you about HR analytics or the validity and reliability of psychometric instruments, you should have an idea of what I'm talking about.

Psychology 101

Sorry, but if you are in HR, you should also have a background in Psychology. And not the kind of psychology used on dating sites. You are dealing with people. You should understand how people think. Their motivations. Their blind spots. Psychology can help with that. I started off with a degree in Psychology, and then found my way into HR. A big part of my work is psychological. It has been of great benefit to me and can be to you as well.

Plus with psychology, you can read people's minds.. well, not really.

Too Administrative

This is the main reason I ran away when I was given the opportunity to become an HR Manager. Those forms. All that paperwork. The bureaucracy. There has to be a better way. The paperwork takes so much time that it leaves time for little else. Who has time to go on a course, or learn the business, when there is a backlog of performance appraisals to be completed from last year? Who has time to gain professional certification, when the intern corrupted the leave data? In this time of technology, HR is way too paper-driven in many companies. Get an assistant. Or outsource it. Or just stop doing it.

The CEO wants people who can give good advice. Advice that they can trust and use. HR has always played a role there but can do a lot more. Paying attention to, and addressing some of the issues raised above can help in that regard.

The Future of Work- this time with HR.

February 5, 2015

Recently I wrote a piece of the future office, where the role of the HR department was all but non-existent. I wanted to further the discussion by showing how HR would function in this environment, where many of the traditional HR functions are handled by the department head, or is outsourced.

In this not so distant future, there is very little mention of the term 'human resources', but you will hear terms like 'talent', 'engagement' and 'efficiency' a lot.

So here is the future office from the HR perspective...

My title says that I'm the Chief Talent Officer- and my role is to ensure that our employees are happy at work so that our customers will be happy to do business with us.
This means a few things:

- *Ensuring that they have the resources to get the job done*

- *Ensure that their time is used effectively at work so that they can maximise the organisation's time (and theirs, by extension)*

- *Find new and creative ways to reward goal achievement*

As CTO, I sit with the CEO to work through business issues. My job is to focus on three things throughout these discussions:

- *How does this impact our employees?*

- *How does this impact our customers?*

- *How does this meet our Vision and Mission?*

It is my responsibility to take these things into account on all business decisions and relay that to the rest of the management team.

Other than an executive assistant, I have no direct reports. Recruitment and payroll functions are managed externally.

Each manager is directly responsible to me for the KPIs related to our People Principle goals. The performance indicators for each employee has three sections:

- *Departmental goals- those related to their job responsibilities*

- *Competence goals- those related to traits we have identified as important to work here*

- *Training goals- those related to acquiring and sharing skills related to the first two areas.*

Departmental Goals

These are fine-tuned every year as part of the strategic planning process. Each year we have one main strategy session, followed by quarterly update sessions. Here we define the goals for each department, and each manager is responsible for breaking them down and assigning them to each member of staff in their area. The target must be measurable, and it goes on the employee's dashboard.

Competency Goals.

This is where we measure things like leadership and teamwork. However, the definitions of these competencies are specific to our company and reflect what it means in our culture. Each competency has specific examples, which act as a guide. This also goes on each employee's dashboard.

***Training goals.** Based on the achievement of the goals in their dashboard, and the current and future needs of the organisation,* *employees have the option of different training programs. These programs have been vetted and approved by the Training Team (which consists of myself, the Finance Manager and the Operations Manager), and includes not only work-related training but competency-based training as well. Employees are expected to share their learning formally after training and are rated on it as part of their review.*

That is our performance management system.

All of the metrics are loaded onto our Intranet and can be updated by employees, their supervisors and managers. Employees are encouraged to nominate each other for 'Spot Awards', where if you spot some doing something that exemplifies the company's vision, they can be rewarded. The metrics are all managed digitally in real time, so all stakeholders have a view of performance, and corrective action can be taken early.

Being active is also an essential part of our corporate culture, and last year the CEO ordered activity trackers for all members of staff. Various competitions are run throughout the year, and employees can gain additional points for activities outside of working hours.

Work/Life balance *is also very important to us. We believe that working late is a sign of inefficiency, not dedication. As such a great emphasis is placed to making sure that each department has adequate resources to function, whether it is personnel or equipment. Processes and procedures have also been established* *for all core processes, and are periodically reviewed for efficiency. To ensure that balance is achieved, all workstations and the lights in the building are set to shut down one hour after the end of the workday. Employees are not allowed to take their laptops home unless there is an emergency situation. All work related calls that come in after hours are routed to the help desk, managed by our on-call staff. Details are taken, and a work request is forwarded to the manager for action. If too many after-hour work requests come in for a particular department, it is addressed at a senior level.*

We believe that spending time away from work and being engaged in other leisure activities with friends and family help to make a more productive, and happy employee.

We have established a few satellite offices, where some employees can work off-site. The idea is that instead of spending many hours commuting on the roads, groups of employees can work together closely to where they live. We are not necessarily in favour of individual employees working from home- collaboration is more difficult. Instead, groups of 3-5 employees, from different departments can use our hot spots to get work done. This is especially useful for our marketing reps, which spend a lot of time on the road.

All sub-offices and overseas locations have a direct video link to Head Office, so in addition to using the phones, employees can walk up to the screen, and chat/have meetings with coworkers and customers alike or access them through their dashboard.

Face to face meetings is also important. Managers are encouraged, through KPIs, to have regular meetings with staff members, to discuss issues related to meeting their objectives. Part of the time is also allocated towards planning and executing team building initiatives.

So HR does fit in- though it may no longer be referred to by that name.

The Future Office- with No Office.

February 20, 2015

I am of the firm belief that is is difficult (if not downright impossible) to be continually innovative and creative in an office environment. Think about it, you spend most of your day in the same space, with the same people, the same colour on the walls and the same paper on your desk. And let's not talk about all the rules and procedures... all those years after the Industrial Revolution, the typical office is no more than a corral for sheep.

The office of the future can't be that way.

To put it in perspective, let me give some personal examples. The times when I am (or feel) the most creative do not usually coincide with the time that I am behind my desk. It usually occurs within minutes of waking up on mornings (early riser), or while I'm on a run or my bike. My creativity especially flows when I am on an overseas trip, experiencing a new place and culture. What tends to happen is that I go to the office to document, and work on these ideas, but rarely am I inspired there.

If your place of work is just that place where you get stuff done, then I guess this does not matter. But if you see your work as a catalyst for other things, then read on.

So can we do away with the office? Probably not. But we can do away with the traditional idea of an office.

After leaving the typical office environment to start my own business, it took me a while- years, in fact, the become unaccustomed to that environment. I still have moments. After spending close to ten years sharing a space with others, it was a bit difficult to make the transition. I had often found that it was difficult to get work done during 'office hours' because of all the distractions (phones, silly meetings, co-workers etc.), so I tended to either work late or take work home. That made little sense- at least to me. The whole point about the office scenario, is so that we would be more productive, right?

Working from home, as I do now (and have for the past six years) is no walk in the park either. There can be other more sinister distractions (like house-work and the bed), as you telecommuters out there would know. There is also the trap of working more hours when at home, as you are less affected by what is going on in the office environment. Is there a happy medium?

So again, a personal example. The biggest shift I had to make was with the concept of working hours. In an office environment, you are expected to be in that physical space for a certain amount of hours to facilitate business. This is especially important in a client facing business. After setting up my home office, I felt the need to maintain 'regular office hours'. It didn't go well. The nature of my work meant that sometimes there was an over-abundance of things to do, and at other times, not much. I felt I was cheating when I had downtime during the 'work day', or had to burn the midnight oil to get a project done.

Then I came to the first realisation of the Future Office- There are no working hours- only hours.

When people ask me nowadays about by work schedule, my standard response is, 'I'm always working'. And it's true. Once I am awake and lucid (they don't always go together), I am working. This holds true whether I am at my desk, at the grocery store or running a half marathon. How does that work? It's easy- my work is synonymous with what I enjoy doing, so in one sense it does not feel like a burden or a chore. Secondly, I don't limit my thoughts, ideas and work to a specific time or place- it flows. So whether I'm waiting for the kids at their after-school activities, or stuck in traffic, my mind can wander from work to non-work issues pretty seamlessly.

The second realisation of the future office is that Technology frees us from the shackles of the desk/office.

Once I have access to the internet, from any device, I can work, and treat with work matters. This means I can start work at 4 am, stop at 6- start back at 10, and finish at 12. And I can be at the park, or the mall, on a plane, or at a client's office. The physical space becomes largely irrelevant. This can also be a double-edged sword, where you work (or are accessible) all the time. But this is easily managed. There are times during the day when I'm taking a break, and I just don't answer my phone or check my e-mail for a couple of hours.

The World is yet to end. At other times, I'm checking e-mails and working on documents at 2 am because I can't get back to sleep. It can work because I don't HAVE to be in a specific place at 8:00 am in the morning. It works.

The next realisation of the future office relates to the office space itself, and the fact that it should inspire you. This is difficult to do when an interior designer outfitted your office. In my office, apart from my desk, filing cabinet and the usual office equipment, I also have my bike and a wall full of all the bibs from races I've done, medals received, and pictures of me in said races.

I can just look up and be reminded of the things that I enjoy doing. And it helps. So the concept of the future office is to focus a lot less on the physical space and to focus more energy on finding a 'mental space' where work and life can happen simultaneously. The issue of work/life balance becomes irrelevant because life does not stop when we go to work, and restart when we leave. And the work itself does not have to be a chore that causes stress. A lot of that work-related stress can be attributed to the physical work environment- and not the work itself.

We will get there, someday.

Presentation for the 11ᵗʰ Human Resource Management Association of Trinidad & Tobago Conference, 2017

As far as trends go, the term 'big data' has been around for a while. Generally speaking, it refers to *data sets that are so large and complex that traditional data processing application software is inadequate to deal with them.*

In this instance, we are referring to *the use of predictive analytics, user behaviour analytics, or certain other advanced data analytics methods that extract value from data, and seldom to the size of the data-set.* In other words- HAVE DATA? USE EXCEL.

The fact is, all HR departments have a large amount of data that is gathered from day to day operations. These include:

1. Time and attendance data
2. Recruitment and Separation statistics
3. Data related to training exercises
4. Incident reporting
5. Performance Management data (including Performance appraisal scores)
6. Psychometric and aptitude test scores
7. Assessment Centre data

All of the above examples are quantitative- they come down to numbers. As a result, they can be used to make predictive assumptions about a group- namely the employees of your organisation. If you have enough data and have been consistently collecting it over a period, there are many, many great things that can happen as a result.

For one, an HR department can use this data to do any of the following:

1. Predict the high and low productivity times of a given year or month
2. Forecast the training budget for the next 2-3 years
3. Work out retention and separation rates by department
4. Figure out why the production department has been missing their targets.

The last one may seem odd, but much of what HR can- and should be doing is a matter of statistics. With the right data set, HR can add significant value to management meetings- beyond the telephone usage report. And when various data sets are combined, the possibilities become endless. For instance, time and attendance data, when combined with data from marketing reports and sales figures- can not only tell you who are the star performers in the Marketing department, but also what time of month (or year) is best for sales. Why is that important for HR? Well, you need to ensure that those members of staff are well compensated and that the relevant (and competent) support staff is in place to support- and extend the effort.

But all of this is only possible if someone is paying attention to the data and collecting it responsibly. And in many cases, HR just does not have the time to do this.

Some of the best data can be found in Psychometric and Assessment Centre data. In many instances, this data is generated by third parties (consultants, etc.). Most of the other data is generated internally within the HR department... and isn't used beyond basic management reports.

But what if there was a way to use all of this data collectively, and use the result to predict not only your budgetary allocations but also the HR needs of the organisation for the next three years? It may sound far-fetched, but as has been already established, many organisations are already sitting on a treasure trove of data that is being underutilised!

Worldwide, decisions are increasingly being made with the use of 'Big Data'. Companies such as Google, Amazon and Apple thrive on this. It is about predicting customer behaviour and wants. By looking at past views and purchases, these companies can 'predict' what you would want to buy in the future- and make sure that ads pop up in your web browser, social media feed and email. They also 'create' future trends, based on past wants. Other organisations also have a lot of information/data on their HR practices, and many of them do not use it for any purpose. This data can be quite valuable because if used correctly can give great insight into the human capital within the company, and identify where key gaps are. There has been a significant shift towards mining that data to look for trends that can drive future business decisions.

And this paper intends to show how this can be done.

We will present an analysis of the psychometric data for some individuals who have undertaken a psychometric assessment as part of either recruitment or development activities conducted by Beyond Consulting over a specific period. There are two main groups- Supervisors & General Staff and Senior Managers & Executives.

We stripped all the personal and company information from the data, as we were only concerned with what the numbers would tell us about the group as a whole. Some statistical analyses were run on the data sets, some of which will now be presented.

We looked at a total of forty-eight (48) competencies[1]- all related to success in the workplace. Then using the arithmetic mean, we ranked the competencies from strongest to weakest- and made several inferences on the data.

~~A Trend Analysis was also~~ done- which showed the relationship

[1] From the Saville Assessments range of assessments (www.savilleassessments.com)

between the competencies (in other words, the ones that go together). When the mean ranking is applied to that data set, the analysis gets interesting. Let's have a look, shall we?

LIST OF 48 COMPETENCY AREAS

Structuring Tasks	Communicating Information	Directing People	Convincing People
Upholding Standards	Interacting with People	Driving Success	Documenting Facts
Following Procedures	Showing Resilience	Developing Expertise	Empowering Individuals
Processing Details	Adopting Practical Approaches	Providing Leadership	Resolving Conflict
Pursuing Goals	Providing Insights	Generating Ideas	Understanding People
Managing Tasks	Taking Action	Team Working	Embracing Change
Inviting Feedback	Challenging Ideas	Evaluating Problems	Examining Information
Creating Innovation	Building Relationships	Exploring Possibilities	Adjusting to Change
Meeting Timescales	Establishing Rapport	Producing Output	Investigating Issues
Checking Things	Impressing People	Interpreting Data	Valuing Individuals
Developing Strategies	Thinking Positively	Giving Support	Articulating Information
Seizing Opportunities	Showing Composure	Making Decisions	Conveying Self-Confidence

The competencies are without a formal definition, which is important because organisations define these terms in different ways. Leadership is not defined in the same way in across companies and industries, though the main tenets remain the same. This allows companies to get more specific in their definitions, while still testing for the general evidence of the competency.

SUPERVISORS AND GENERAL STAFF- TOP TEN

	Competency	Mean
1	Following Procedures	6.58
2	Developing Expertise	6.09
3	Understanding People	6.07
4	Processing Details	6.05
5	Resolving Conflict	5.91
6	Giving Support	5.80
7	Managing Tasks	5.76
8	Inviting Feedback	5.75
9	Conveying Self-Confidence	5.74
10	Empowering Individuals	5.73

The first thing that you will notice is that many of these competencies are what you would expect in this group. Areas such as **(1) Following Procedures, (4) Processing Details, (7) Managing Tasks** and **(6) Giving Support**, are essential amongst the supervisory ranks and the fact that they are they rank so highly is a good sign.

Of particular interest is **(3) Understanding People**. It is generally understood that employees who are 'closest to the floor' have a better sense of the customer wants and needs (and also bear the brunt of criticism of company policy), and this may be an indication of that.

SUPERVISORS AND GENERAL STAFF- BOTTOM TEN

	Competency	Mean
39	Directing People	4.92
40	Convincing People	4.91
41	Showing Composure	4.89
42	Evaluating Problems	4.86
43	Taking Action	4.81
44	Articulating Information	4.76
45	Documenting Facts	4.73
46	Providing Insights	4.73
47	Communicating Information	4.71
48	Examining Information	4.69

Conversely, when we look at the other end of the spectrum, there are a few of these that we would prefer to be a bit higher in the rankings- for example **(42) Evaluating Problems, (45) Documenting Facts, (47) Communicating Information** and **(40) Convincing People**.

In particular **(39) Directing People** is worthy of note. In this case, many may ascribe this to senior management, and they would be correct- but supervisors spend a considerable amount of time directing and supervising the work of others- usually in a very 'hands-on' and practical way. As such, this is an important competency- and may have to be defined separately for this level. It is an area for some level of focus.

OTHER FACTORS:

While the ranking order may depend on the industry (e.g. companies in the Retail environment may place more value on 'softer', customer-centric skills), there are a few that should be considered crucial across the board.

Let's have a look at a few of them.

19- Team Working: This may also be considered a critical skill at this level, especially in environments where cross-functional teams are necessary to meet the needs of clients. A low score here may also explain why team-working assignments/structures in many organisations fail- culturally, it may not be supported by the organisation.

21- Structuring Tasks: Another area that can be deemed critical, especially in engineering and other specialised industries, and poor quality can adversely affect service delivery- even safety.

29- Building Relationships: Mainly considered a 'soft skill' but critical in customer-facing environments. The employees' ability to build relationships with clients is heavily influenced by company policy and practice- which sometimes gets in the way building mutually beneficial relationships.

31- Generating Ideas: This may also be considered an area for Managers and Executives, however as supervisors and general employees are 'close to the customer' in many cases, their insight in problem-solving and developing customer-friendly processes can provide valuable insight- *in organisations that facilitate it.*

34- Providing Leadership: Another area also traditionally attributed to upper management, but is critical on the 'shop floor.' Organisations that empower employees at the entry levels may be able to address issues before they escalate.

SUPERVISORS AND GENERAL STAFF- TREND ANALYSIS

A trend analysis of the data was also done, in a bid to identify causal relationships between the competencies. The statistical analysis grouped the competencies that had a strong causal relationship to each other- and the group with the most significant relationship is highlighted below:

Competency	Corr.	No.
Driving Success	.875	37
Directing People	.857	39
Providing Leadership	.807	34
Pursuing Goals	.802	26
Seizing Opportunities	.728	36
Making Decisions	.723	38
Taking Action	.682	43
Providing Insights	.619	46
Embracing Change	.516	32

It is important to note that many, if not all of these competencies can be associated with the Management and Executives group. This is instructive if you consider the data from a Succession Planning perspective. Many organisations would hope that, through a series of development initiatives and promotion, that some employees would be able to progress through the ranks into management. These are the employees that the organisation would want to develop and retain. The psychometric data, as well as other measures, are instructive in identifying these persons, but the next step is even more critical.

If this data represented a company or department, it could be used to inform all training and development initiatives for at least the next three years.

Regarding preparing for the training cycle; this information can be looked at in two ways:

1. Current and Critical Training Needs
2. Talent Management and Development

The first level is straightforward. The organisation would choose the critical areas that are in alignment with its core values, and that has led to organisational issues in the past (i.e. through customer complaints, non-conforming service and performance appraisal flags). The information on psychometric assessments adds another objective layer to the process of selecting training needs (since it is filled out by the employees themselves).

HR can now select the competency areas for development, and:

1. Find training courses that are in alignment with them
2. Develop in-house programs such as mentoring and coaching
3. Work with service providers to develop bespoke programs for staff

All of this can be done in advance of the training budget, and inform the budgeting process.

There is also an additional advantage.

HR can create an Employee Profile that can be used in the recruitment process- where new employees are brought in who already possess the skills required.

The second level is also critical.

HR will now be in a position to identify 'employees of interest'- those that would be good candidates for a succession planning program. A separate program could then be developed to fast-track the development of these employees so that the organisation has a cadre of internal candidates for a variety of positions.

This can also be planned and budgeted in advance. At Beyond Consulting, we have some templates and options for this particular type of initiative.

MANAGERS AND EXECUTIVES- TOP TEN

	Competency	Mean
1	Following Procedures	6.57
2	Upholding Standards	6.56
3	Structuring Tasks	6.52
4	Processing Details	6.47
5	Interpreting Data	6.31
6	Managing Tasks	6.31
7	Meeting Timescales	6.23
8	Pursuing Goals	6.21
9	Evaluating Problems	6.21
10	Checking Things	6.20

The first observation, and which should hold some considerable concern, is that several of the competencies outlined in the top ten can be considered to be standard at the Supervisory level, and not at the Manager and Senior Executive level. Competencies such as **(1) Following Procedures, (3) Structuring Tasks, (4) Processing Details** and **(10) Checking Things**, can all arguably be essential at the Supervisory level. More importantly, there are others that one would expect in the top ten that are not there.

MANAGERS AND EXECUTIVES- BOTTOM TEN

	Competency	Mean
39	Convincing People	5.51
40	Taking Action	5.43
41	Showing Resilience	5.42
42	Communicating Information	5.39
43	Building Relationships	5.27
44	Establishing Rapport	5.25
45	Thinking Positively	5.22
46	Challenging Ideas	5.18
47	Impressing People	5.16
48	Showing Composure	5.09

There is even more concern when we look at the composition of the bottom ten. There are a few here that we may reliably expect to have been in the top ten. Competencies such **as (39) Convincing People, (40) Taking Action, (42) Communicating Information, (43) Building Relationships** and **(46) Challenging Ideas**, may have all been on a list as core senior management competencies. The fact that they rank so poorly (in relation to the others) does require further investigation.

MANAGERS AND EXECUTIVES- 'SECOND' TEN

	Competency	Mean
11	Inviting Feedback	6.09
12	Exploring Possibilities	6.04
13	Developing Expertise	6.04
14	Creating Innovation	5.99
15	Developing Strategies	5.91
16	Team Working	5.90
17	Investigating Issues	5.89
18	Documenting Facts	5.88
19	Producing Output	5.86
20	Examining Information	5.83

The data is even more instructive when we expand to the 'Second Ten'. Here, we find several competencies which would also be considered essential at this level, and include **(12) Exploring Possibilities, (14) Creating Innovation, (15) Developing Strategies, (17) Investigating Issues** and **(20) Examining Information.** The fact that they are not lower in the list does provide some consolation, but when mixed with the first ten, there is a sense that some Executives may not have all the skills required to be successful at this level.

There are a few other competencies that are worthy of note:

21- Directing People: This may be expected to be a key component at this level, though some organisations may place a higher premium on it than others.

22- Giving Support and 36- Empowering Individuals: Considered as 'softer skills' and ones that many executives may have it short supply- nonetheless they are important in the development of a cohesive and supportive working environment.

23- Driving Success, 24- Generating Ideas and 28- Seizing Opportunities: With little argument, these would be considered key competencies for an executive. The fact that they rank near the middle of the data set should be a cause for concern.

30- Articulating Information and 37- Making Decisions: Sharing the vision and ensuring its implementation are key aspects of an Executive's working life, and as such should have a higher overall ranking.

MANAGERS AND EXECUTIVES- TREND ANALYSIS

As with the Supervisor group, a trend analysis of the data was done, in a bid to identify causal relationships between the competencies. The statistical analysis grouped the competencies that had a strong causal relationship to each other- and the group with the most significant relationship is highlighted below:

Competency	Corr.	No.
Driving Success	.875	23
Directing People	.857	21
Providing Leadership	.807	31
Pursuing Goals	.802	8
Seizing Opportunities	.728	28
Making Decisions	.723	37
Taking Action	.682	40
Providing Insights	.619	38
Embracing Change	.516	32

And as with the previous group, a number of these competencies should be ranked within the top ten for an Executive. Their ranking on the list shows that some, more than others, require a lot of development.

What would this information reveal, if it were for a particular organisation?

It would suggest that many of the Executives may have been promoted from the supervisory levels, based on length of service, and not necessarily based on ability (competence) to do the job required at the Executive level.

This is of particular concern in the Caribbean- where the pool of prospective candidates is small.

There could be other factors, but such a hypothesis would seem reasonable- especially if tied to the data set for the Supervisors- which in many respects are similar.

So what should an organisation do, when it finds itself with a majority of senior managers and Executives that do not possess the full slate of management competencies? There are three options available that are all linked:

1. **Hire in the Skill:** This is straightforward enough- the psychometric assessment data allows the organisation to 'construct' the perfect executive based on competencies, and each new hire can be compared against that standard. It is essential however that the organisational culture matches the preferences of these new hires, or their stint will be short-lived.

2. **Train, Coach and Mentor:** As identified for the supervisors as well, a more immediate program of training and one-on-one Coaching and Mentoring may be necessary to bring the executives 'up to speed.' Whether done in-house or outsourced, the HR department will have a clear view of the skills that are necessary and can employ the

necessary resources. This can also be budgeted for going forward.

3. **Talent Management Development Program:** The organisation may decide to employ the use of a more formal development program to develop the skill of the Executive Team. This could include 360-degree assessments, Development Centres and some other components designed into a formal Talent Management Program. Such a program could have the lifespan of up to three years and includes continuous development and feedback.

ABOUT THE AUTHOR

Jeremy Francis is the Managing Director/Principal Consultant of Beyond Consulting- a company that focuses on People and Process Development. While working in the HR and Process Improvement fields in a variety of industries, Mr Francis recognised that productivity and efficiency issues within companies are not simply a People or a Process issue, but involve a delicate balance between these two dynamics within an organisation. Beyond Consulting offers services that bridge this gap.

He can be reached at jeremy.francis@beyondconsultingtt.com

www.beyondhappyatwork.com

Other books by the same author:

The HR Genie: *A Guide to Performance Management.*
2015

How to get and Stay Hired: (*Or maybe start your own business*)
2018

www.ingramcontent.com/pod-product-compliance
Lightning Source LLC
Chambersburg PA
CBHW030943240526
45463CB00016B/1739